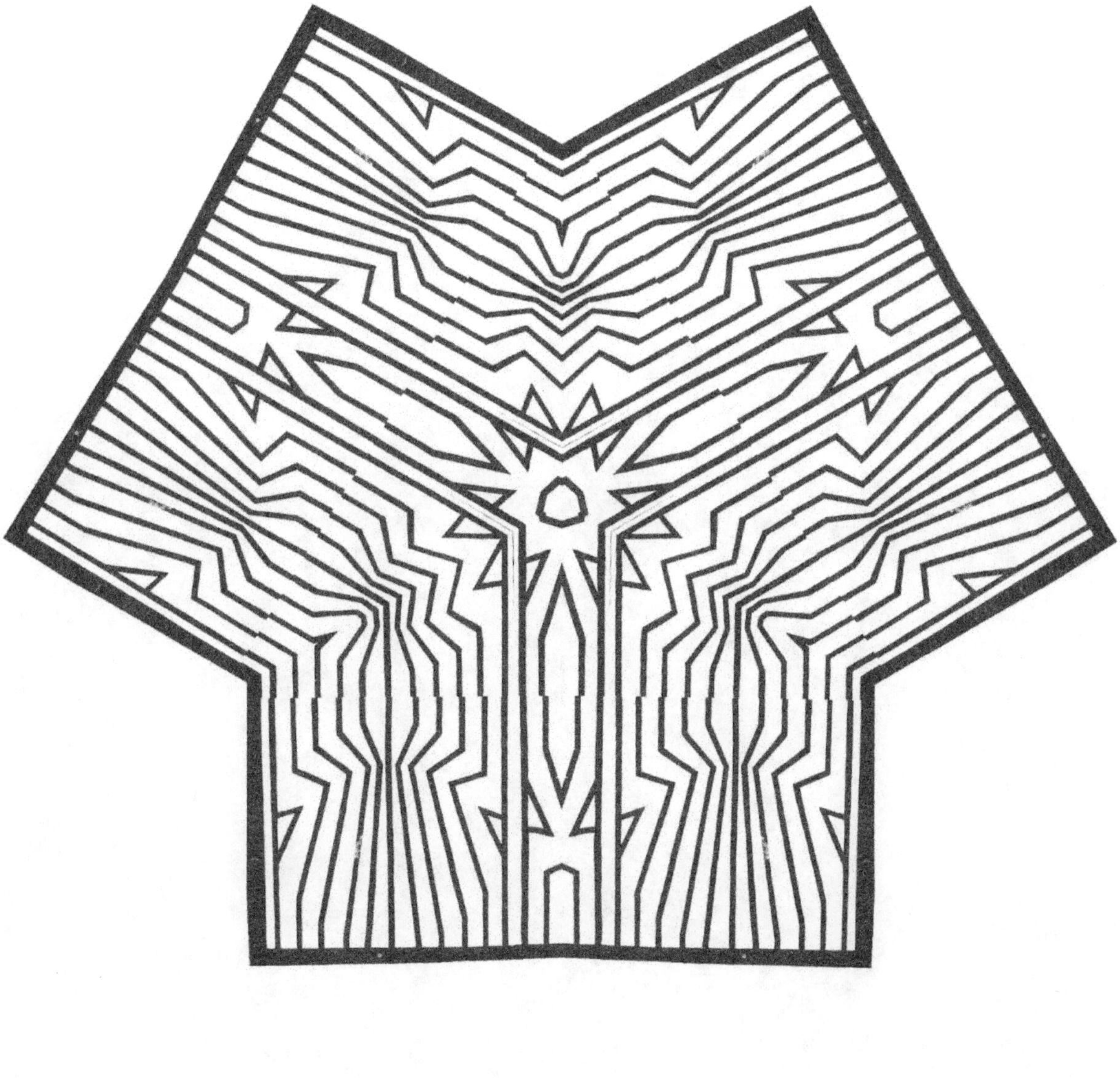

<u>COLORING</u>

AND

<u>*CREATING*</u>

This book was created

for

Children and Adults

Welcome to

Coloring Book for Autistic Children and Adults

Get out your markers, colored pencils, gel pens, or watercolors!

You might want to place a sheet of paper or thin cardboard behind the design before you begin to color. This will catch any possible bleeding through of color.

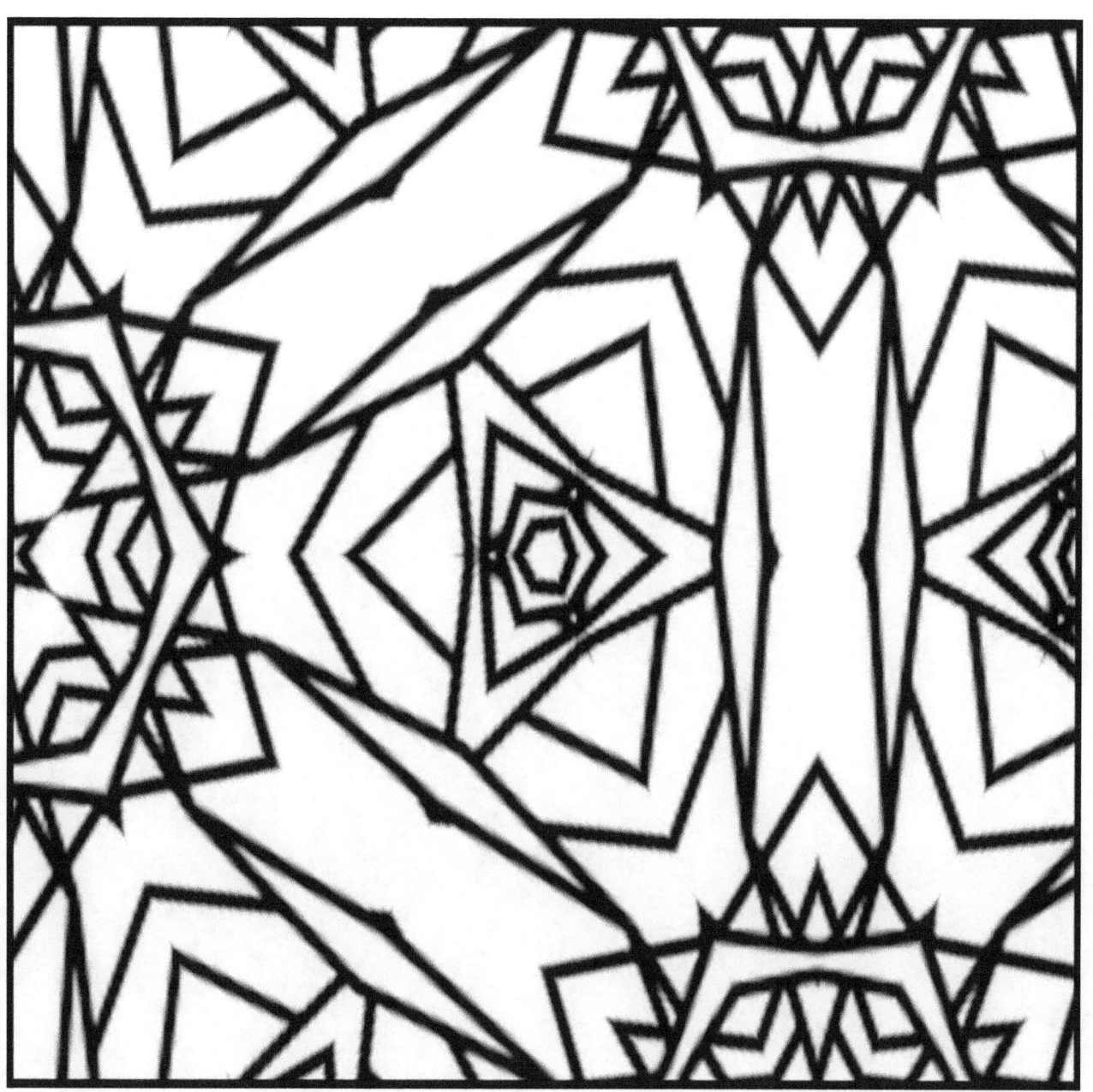

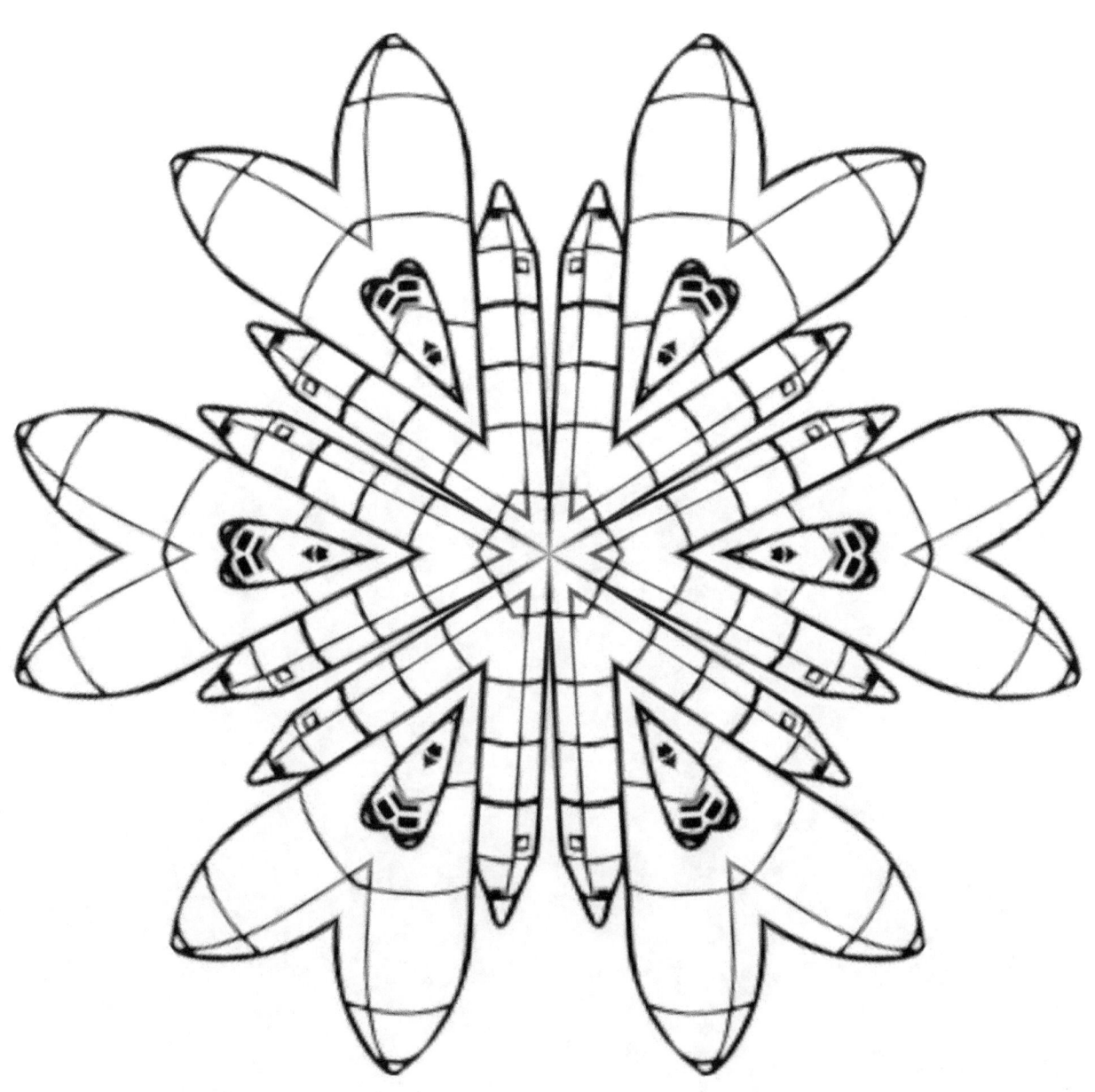

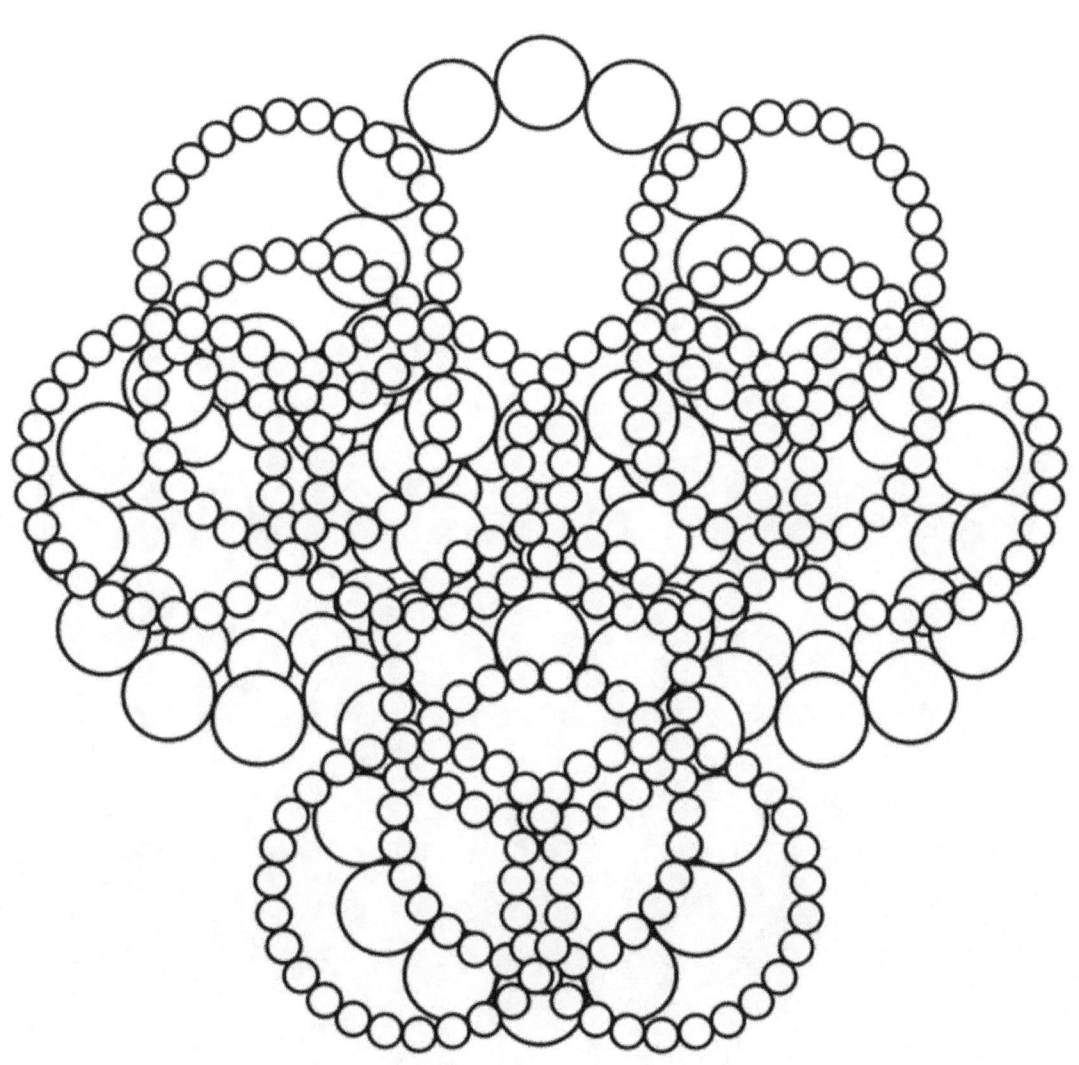

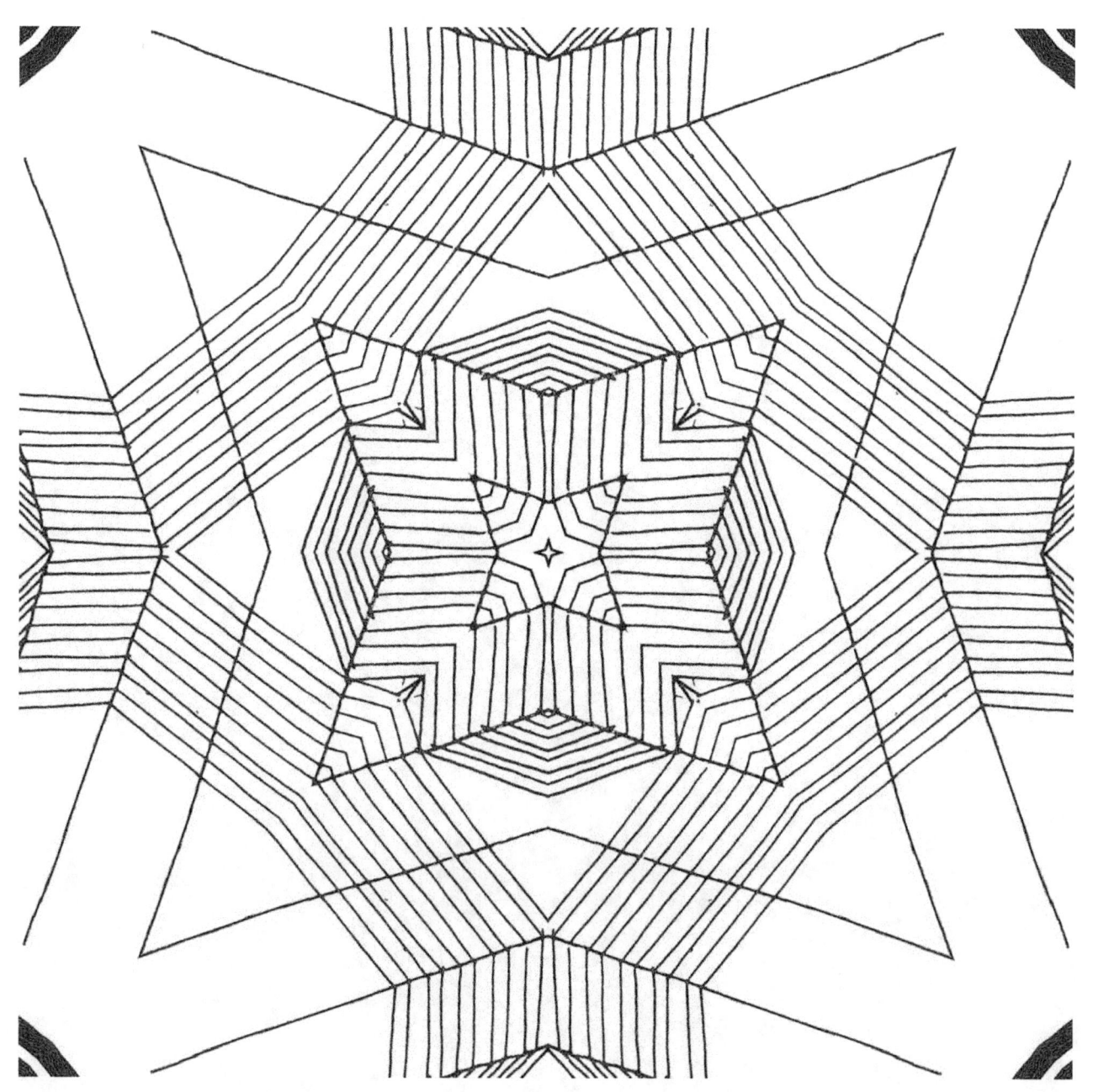

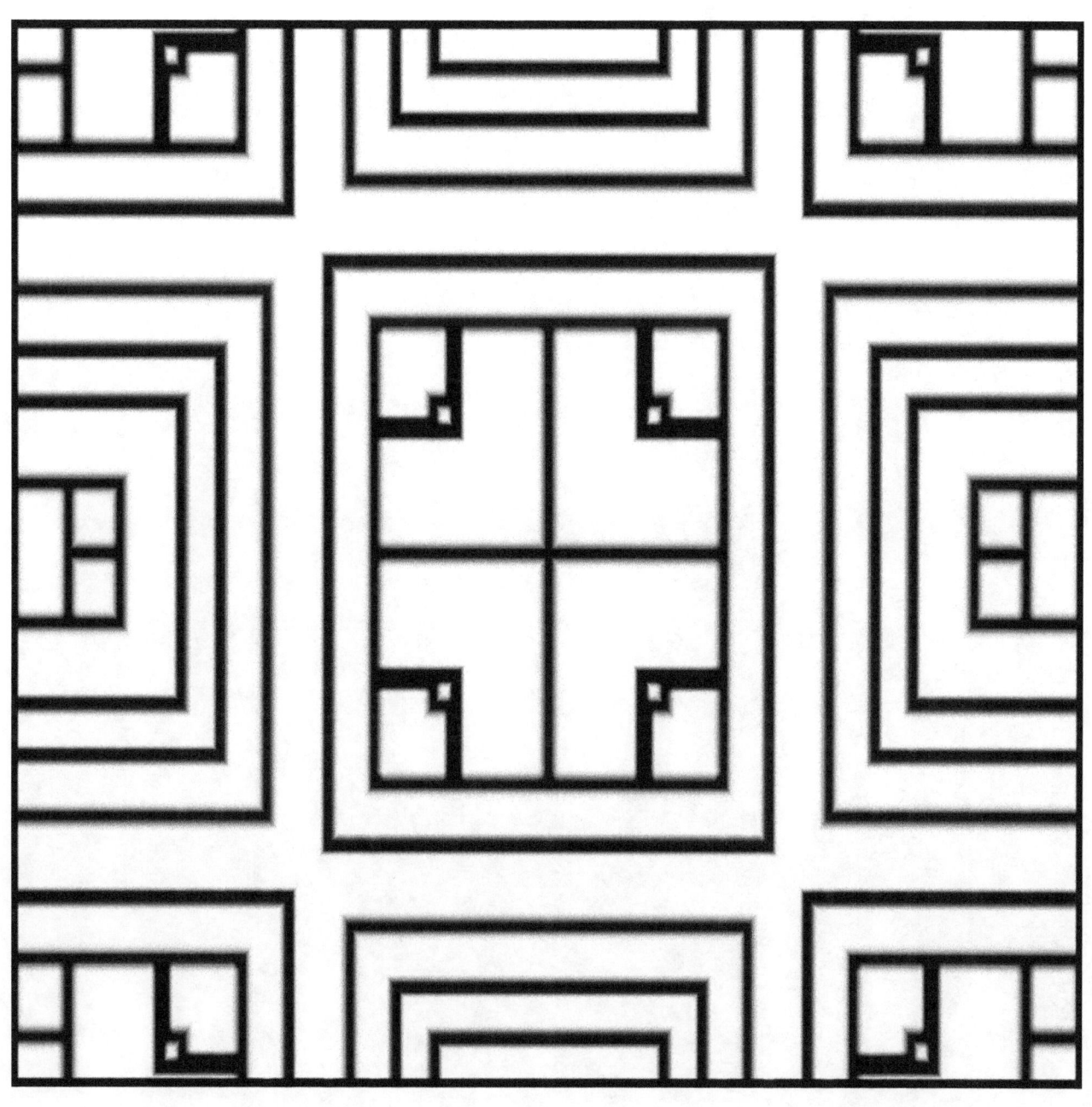

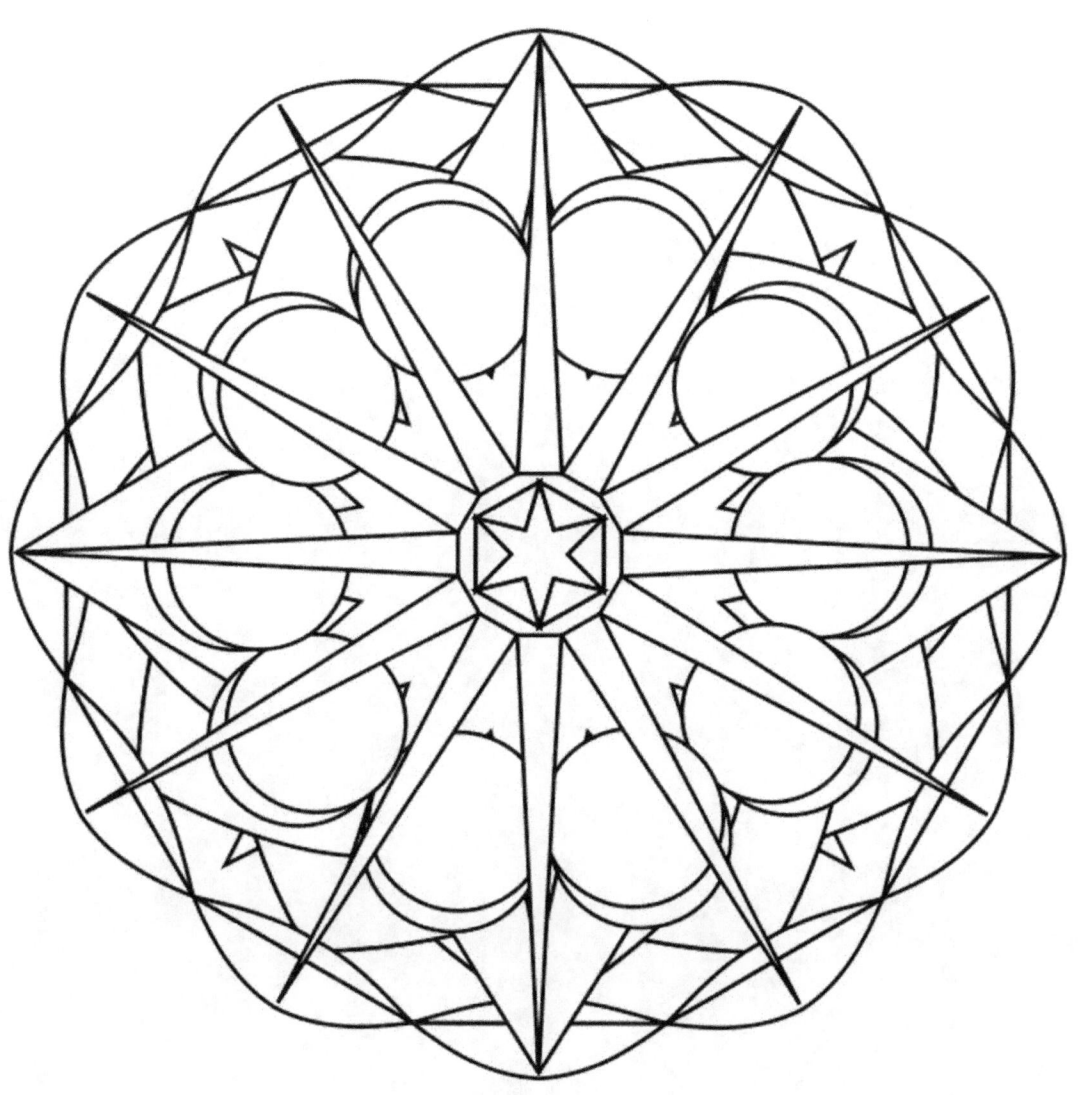

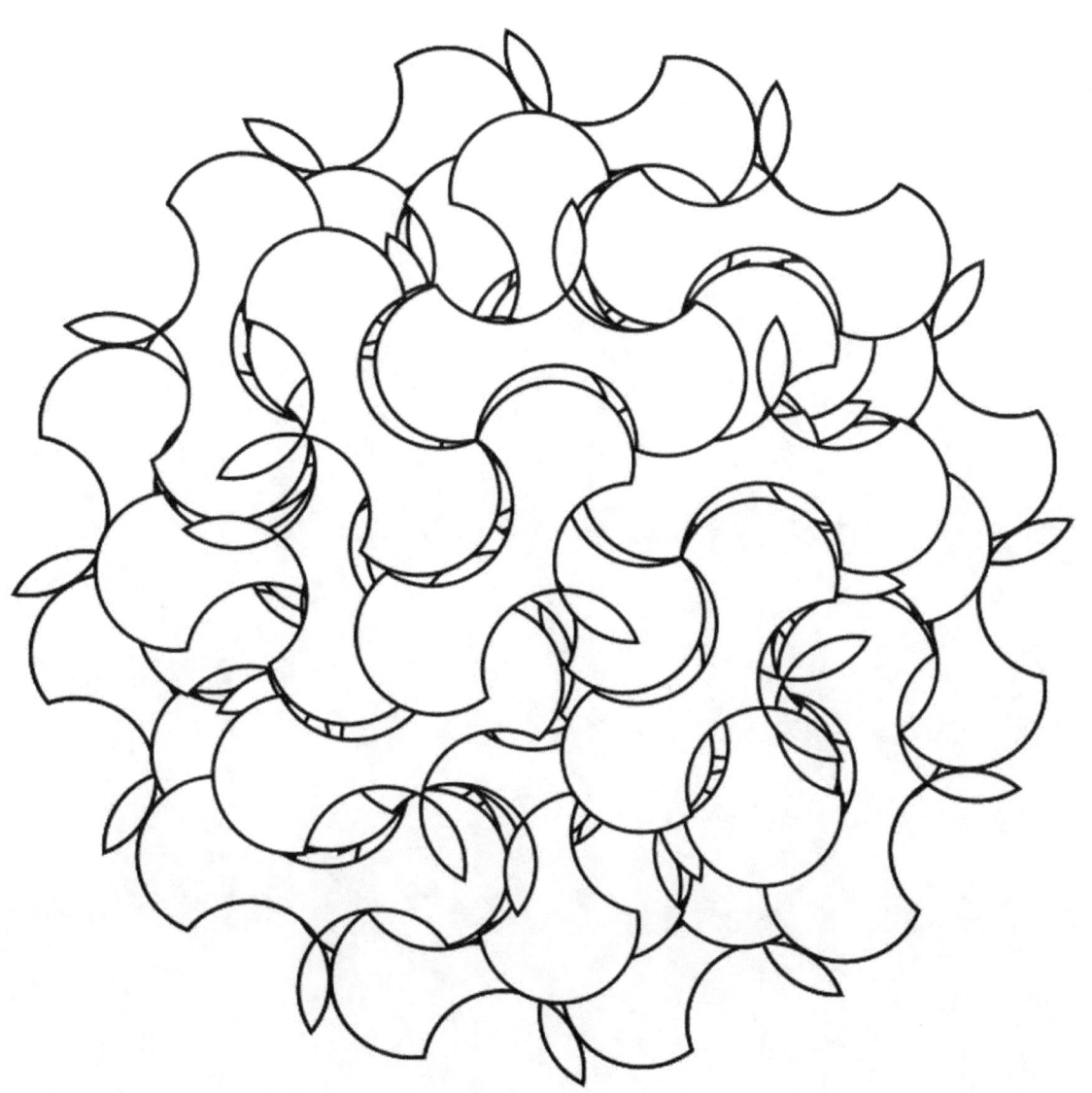

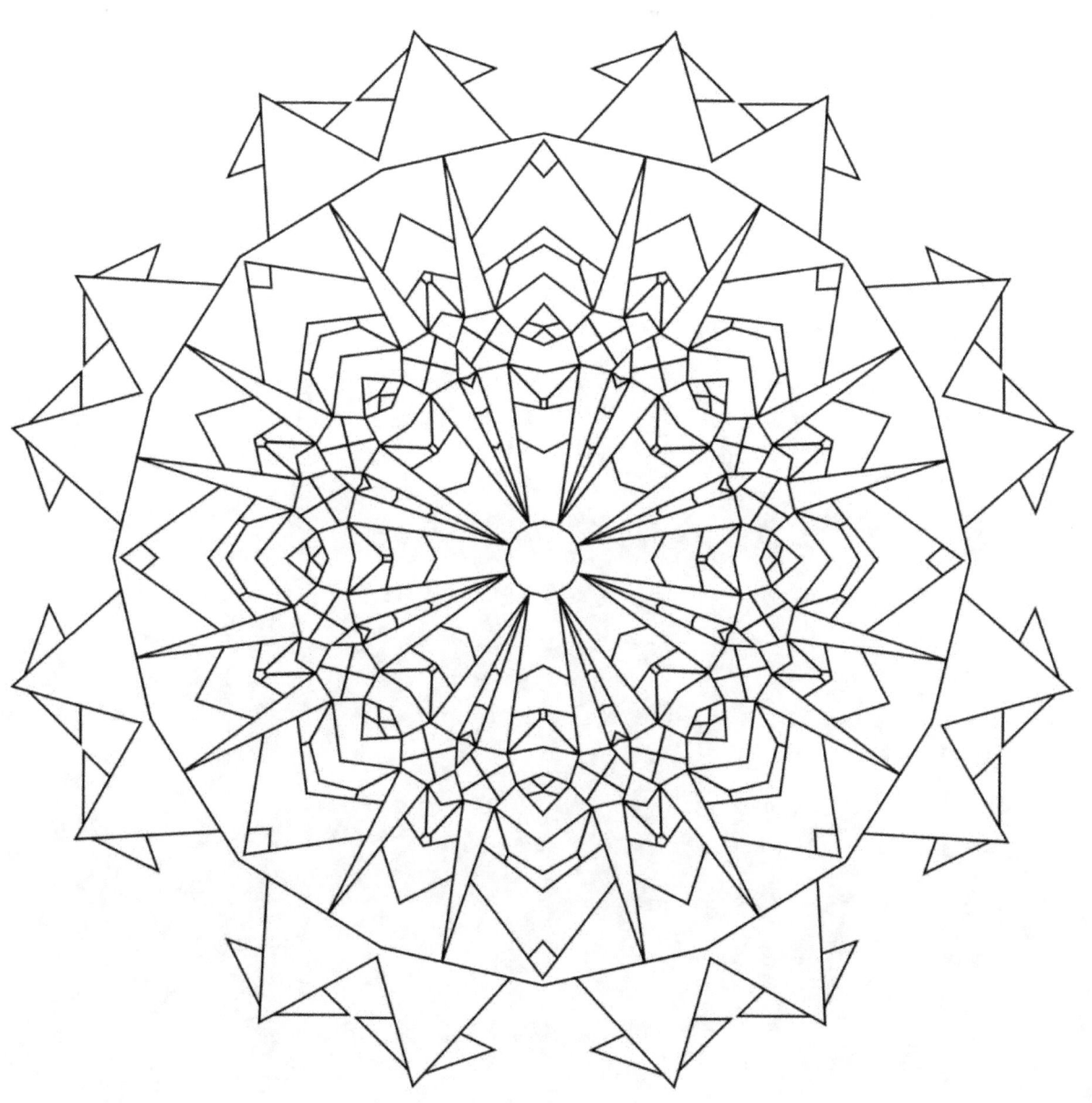

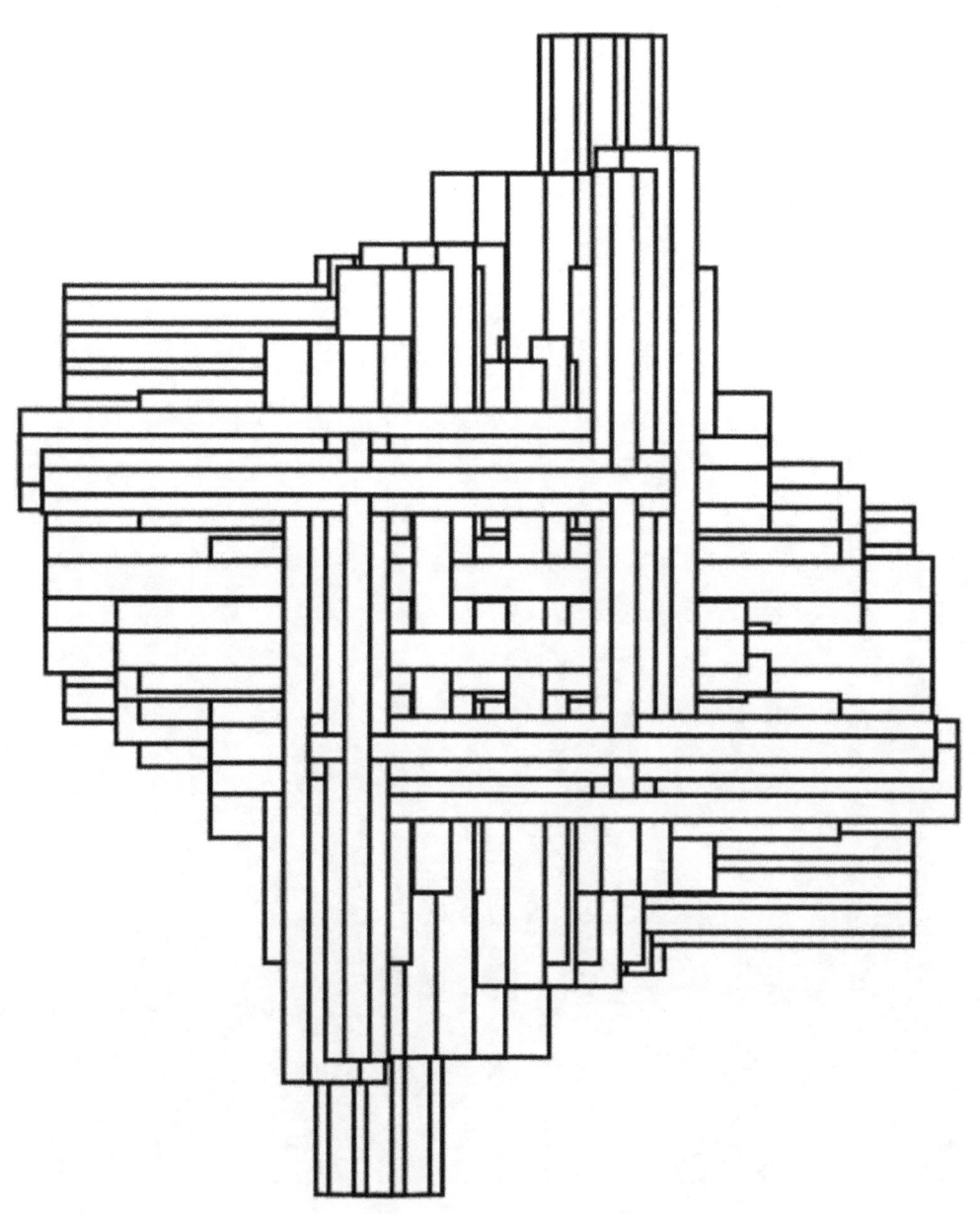

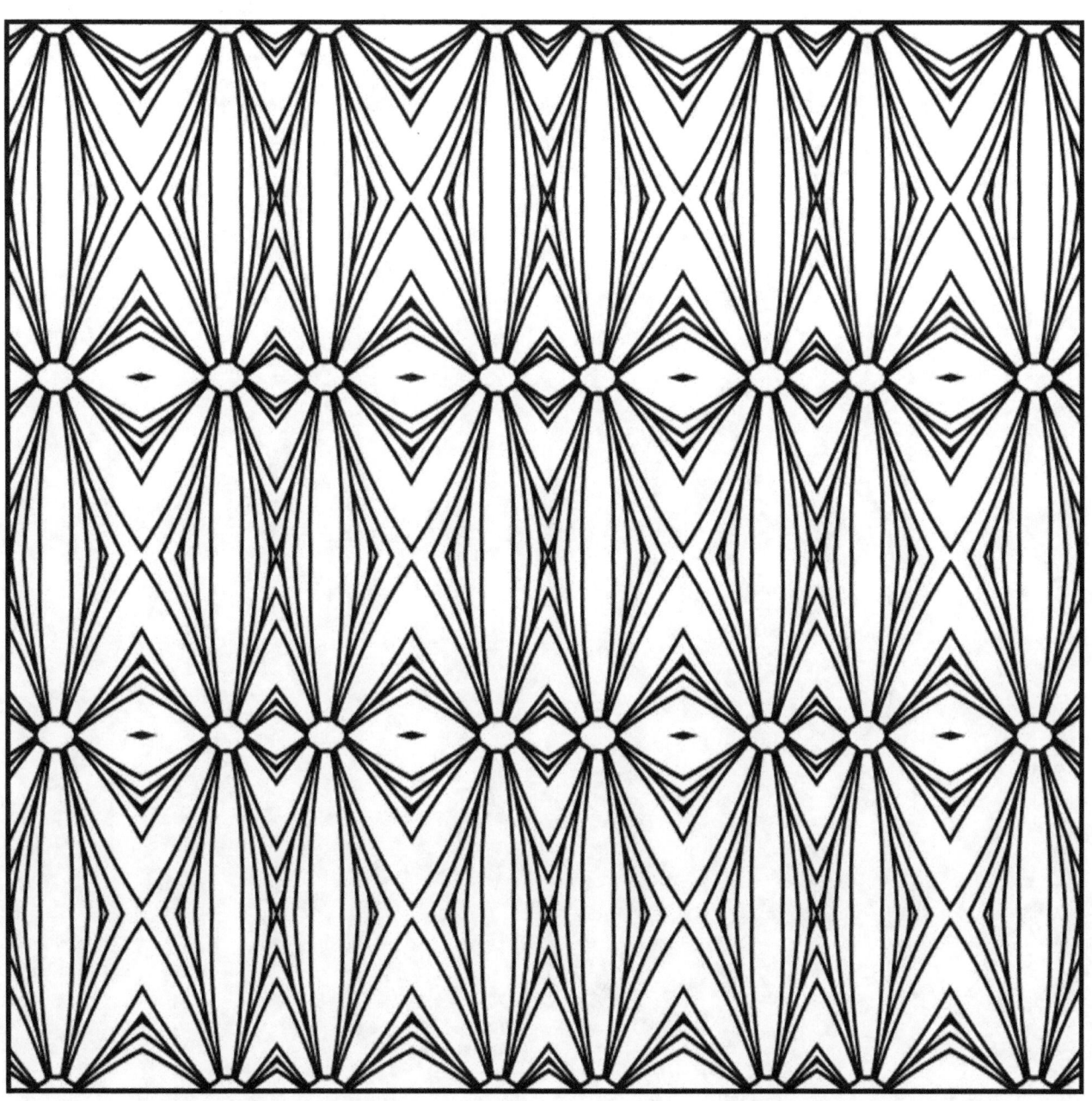

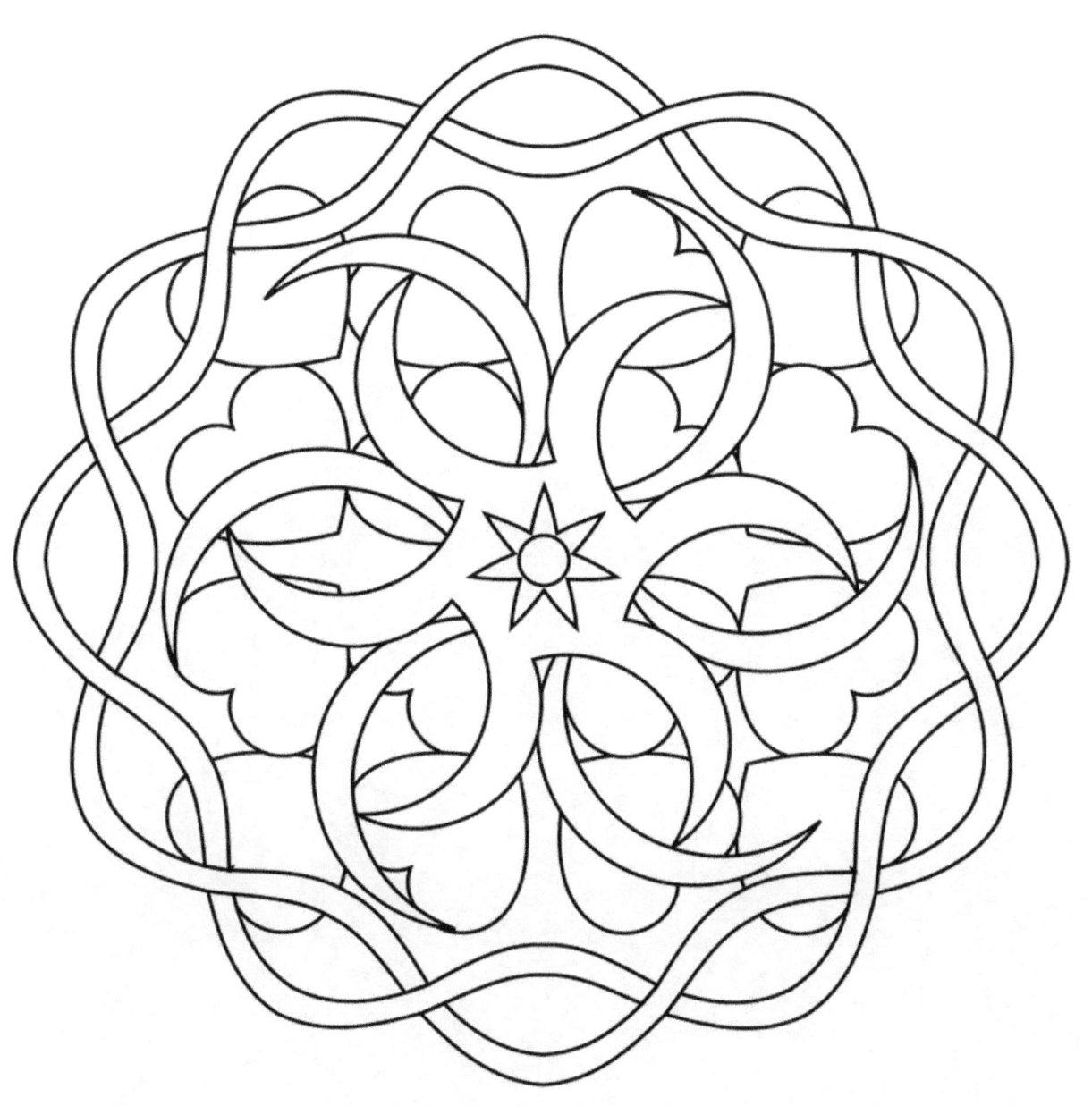

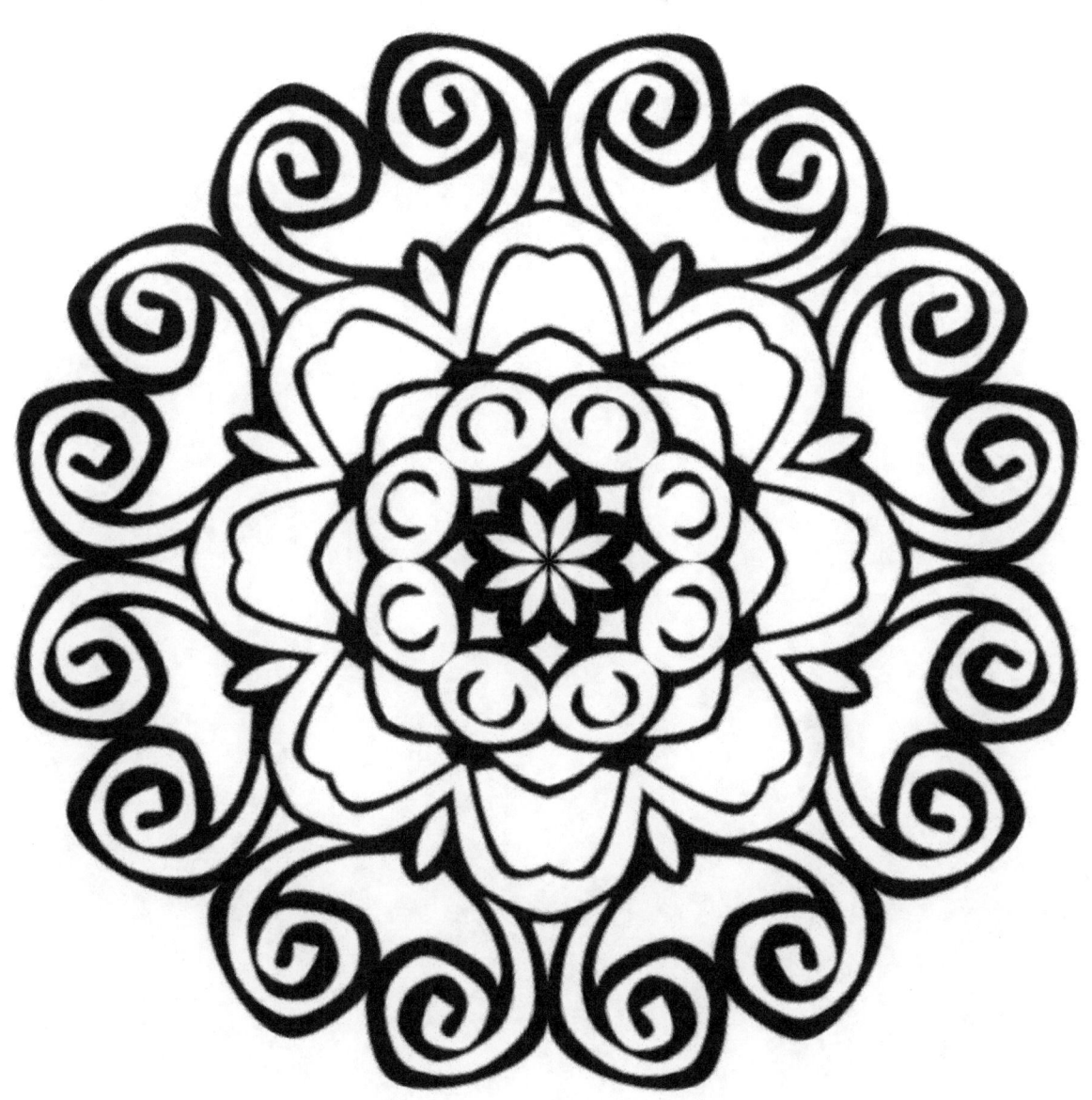

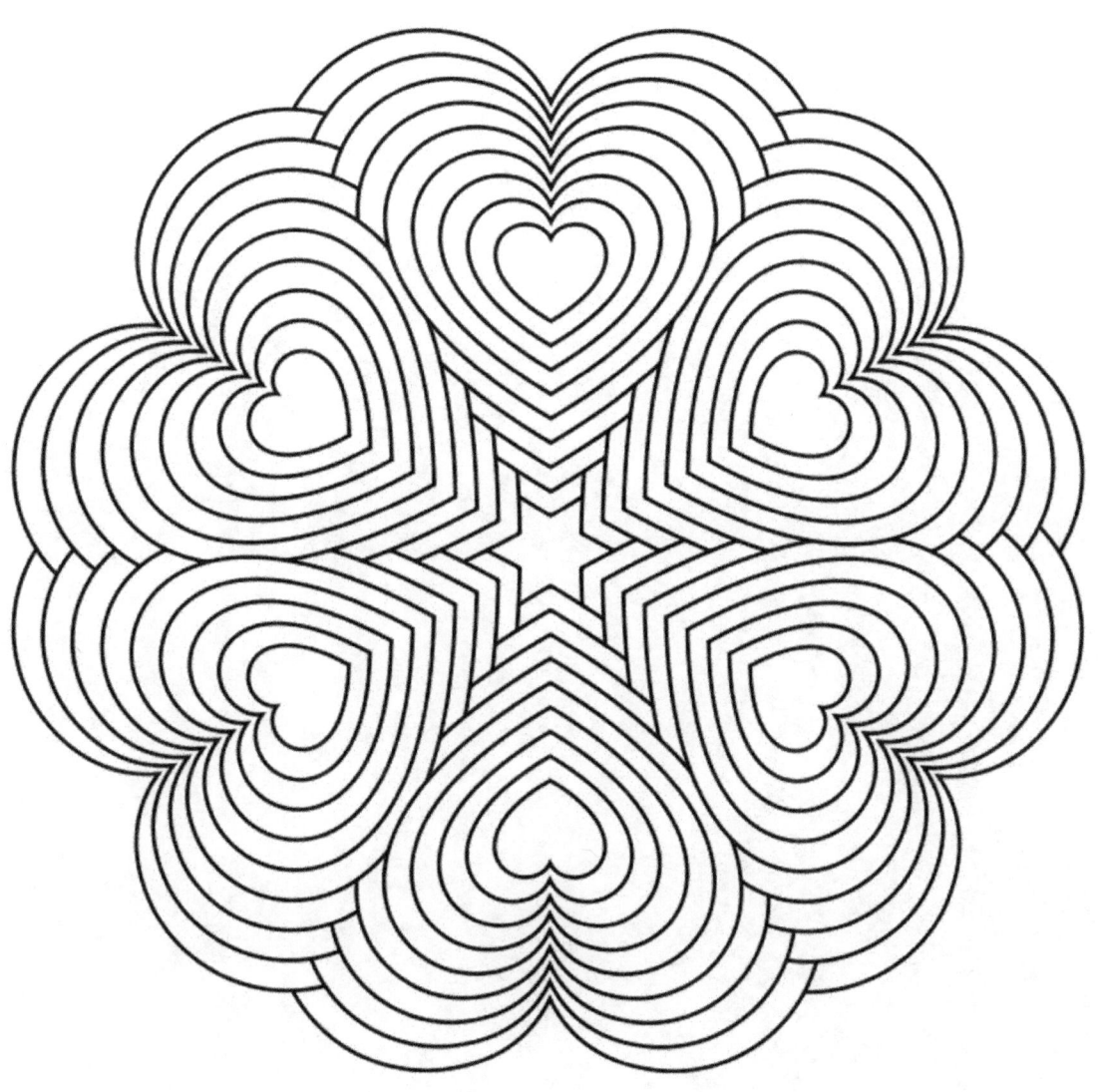

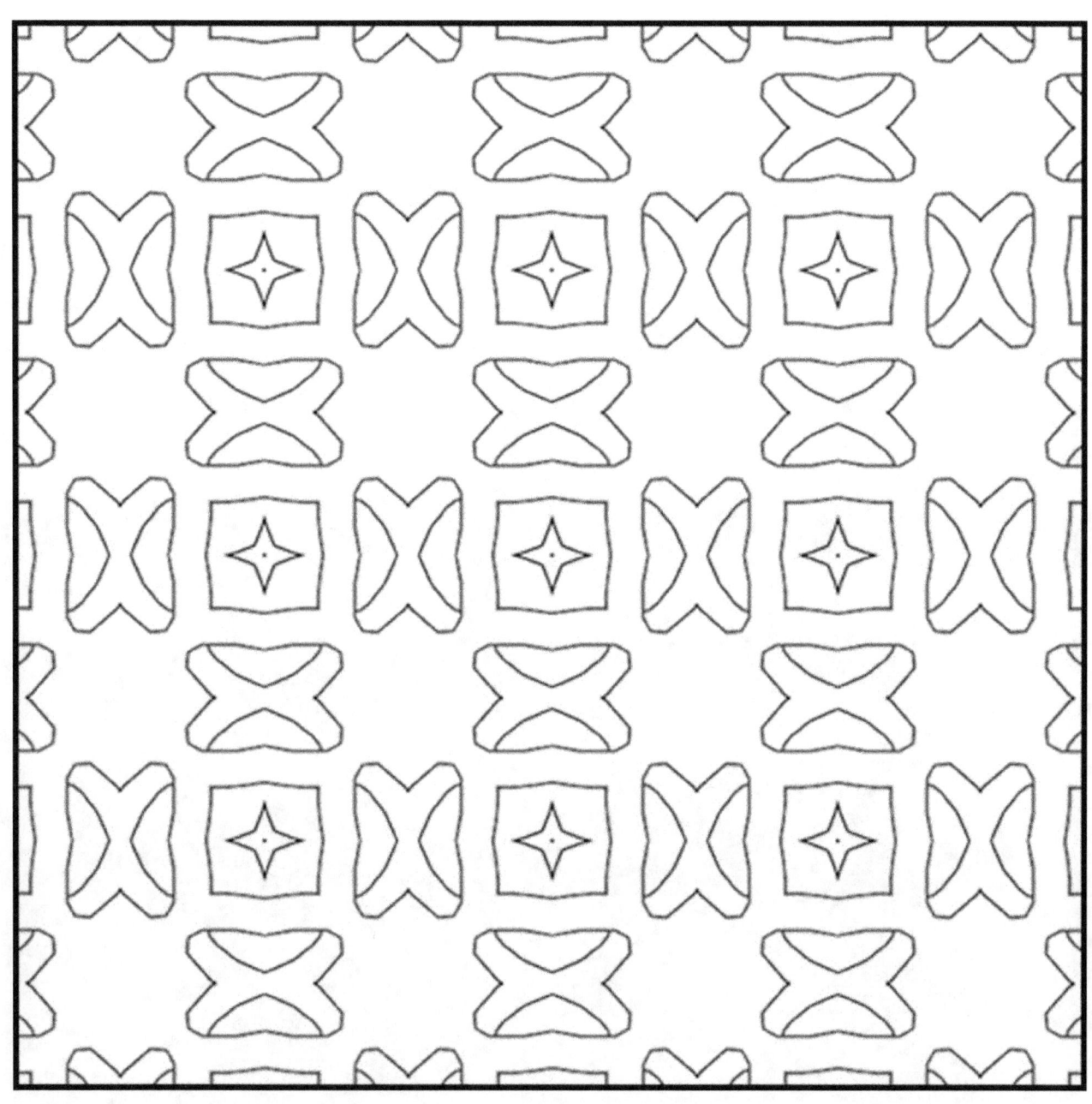

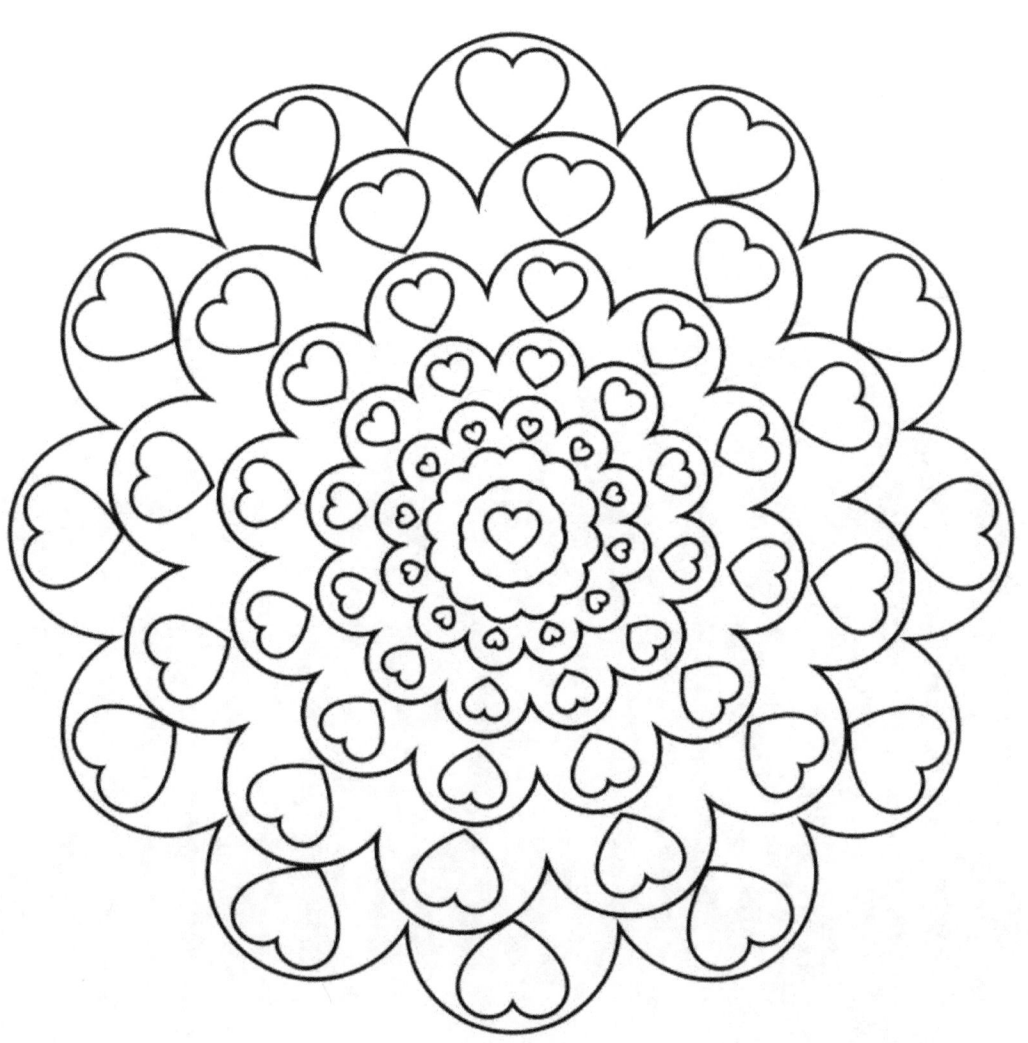

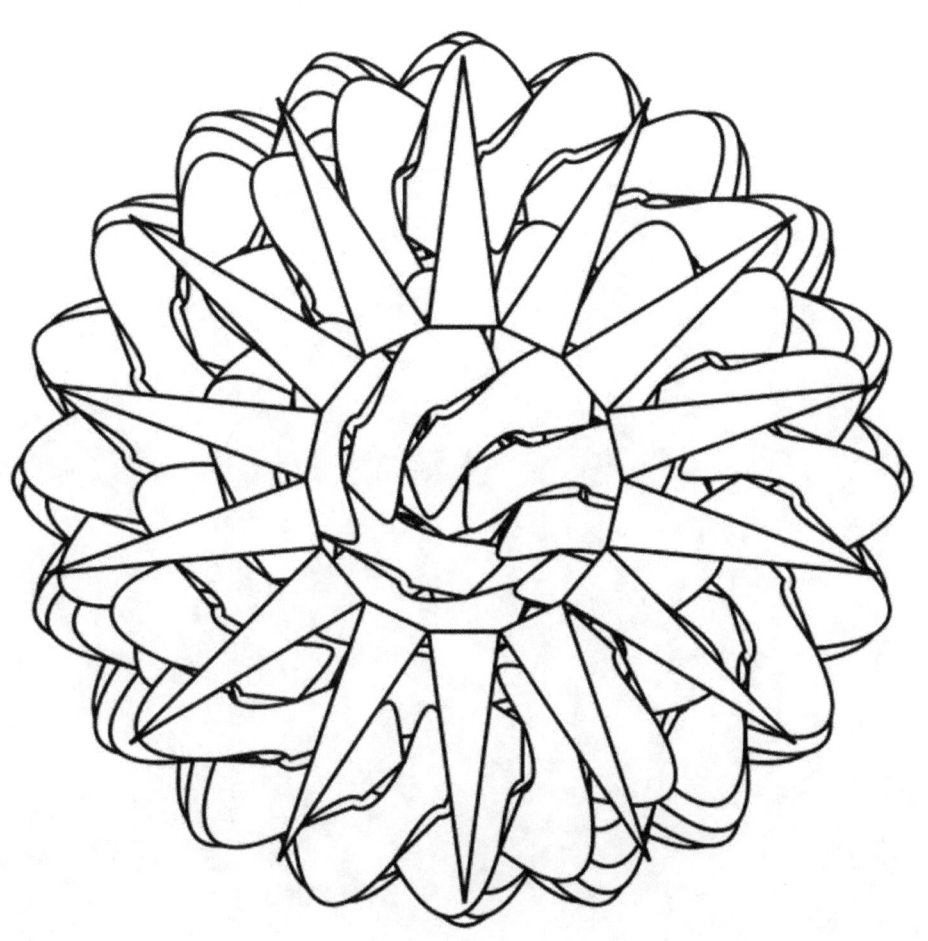

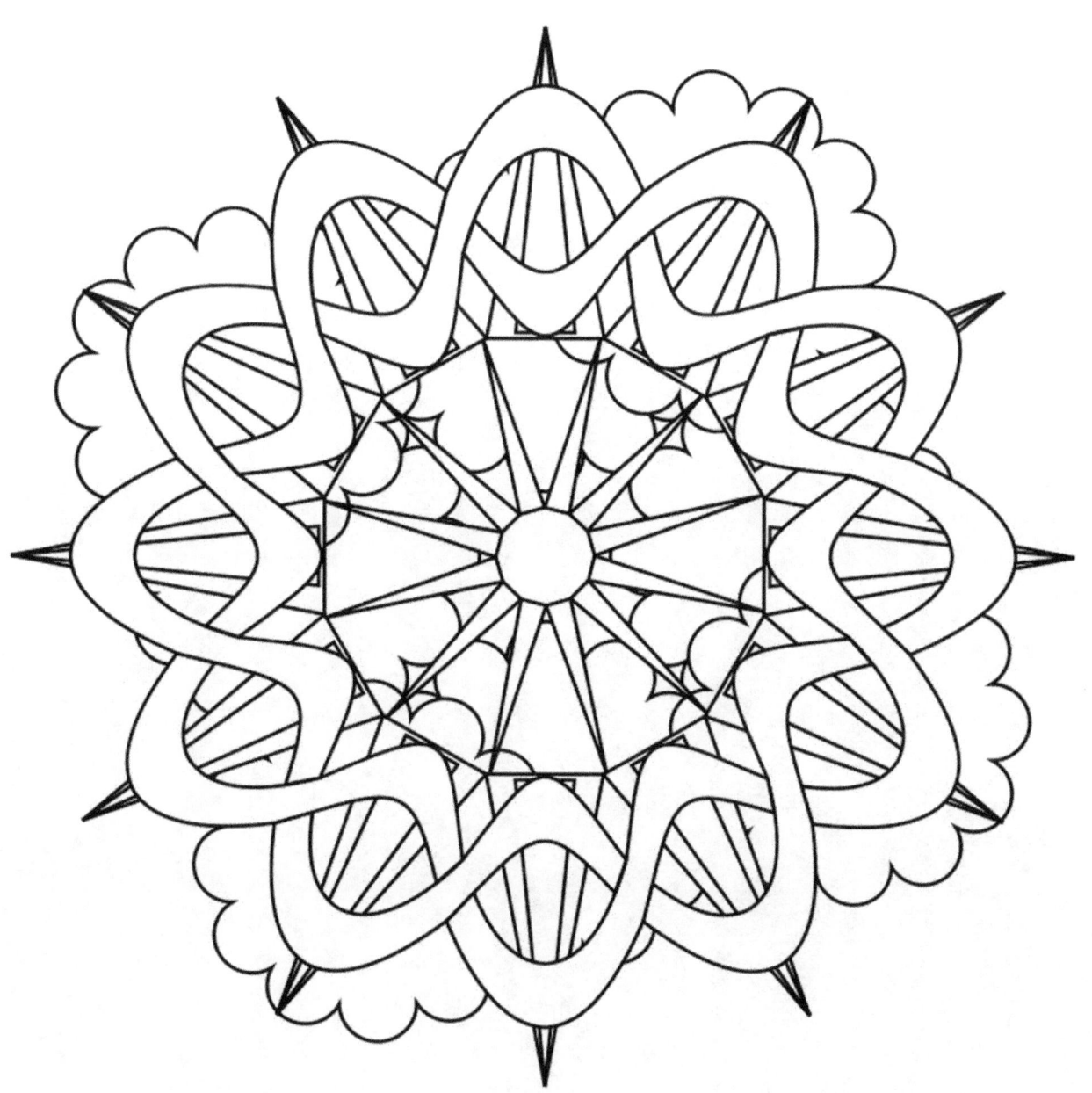

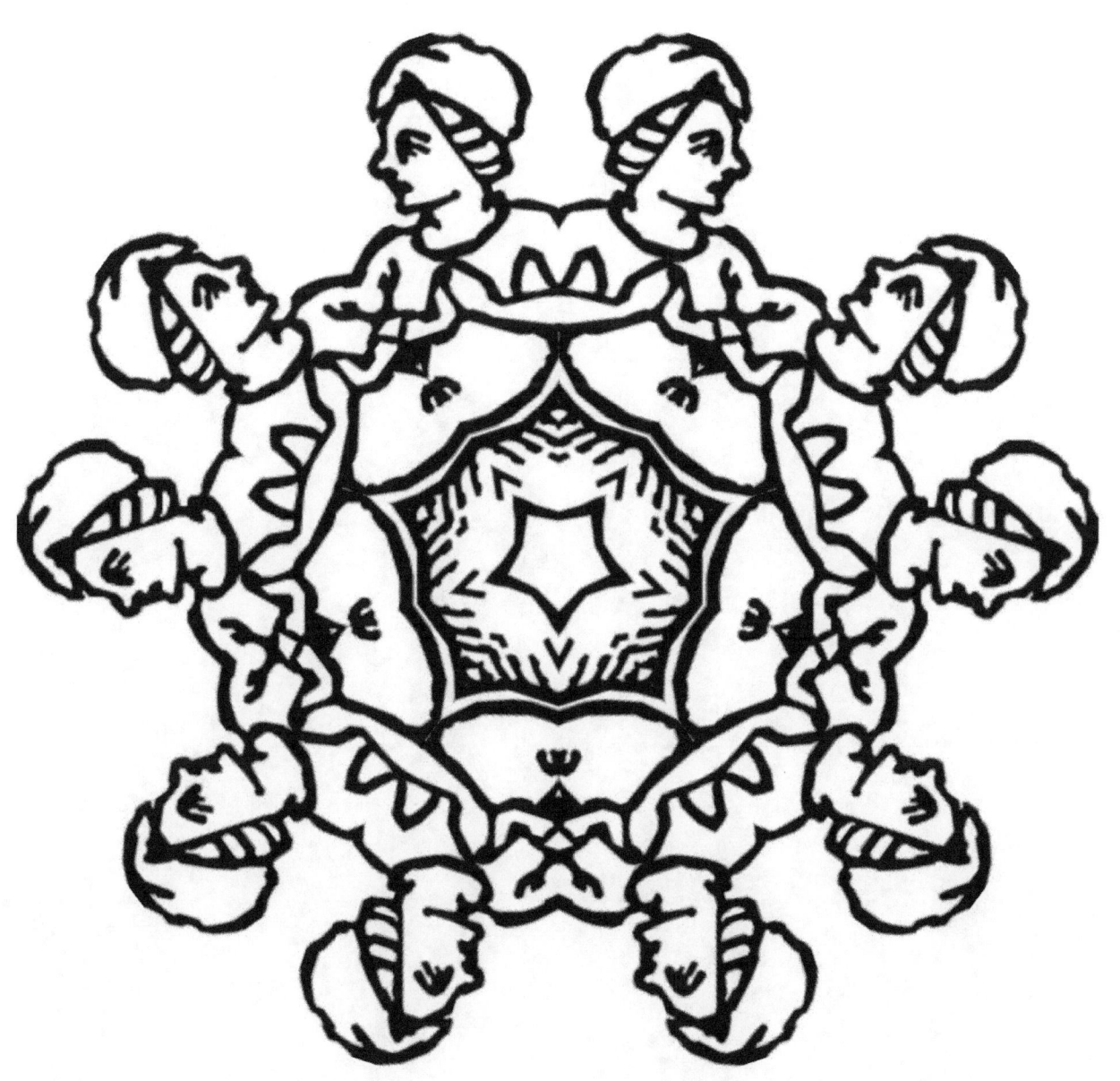

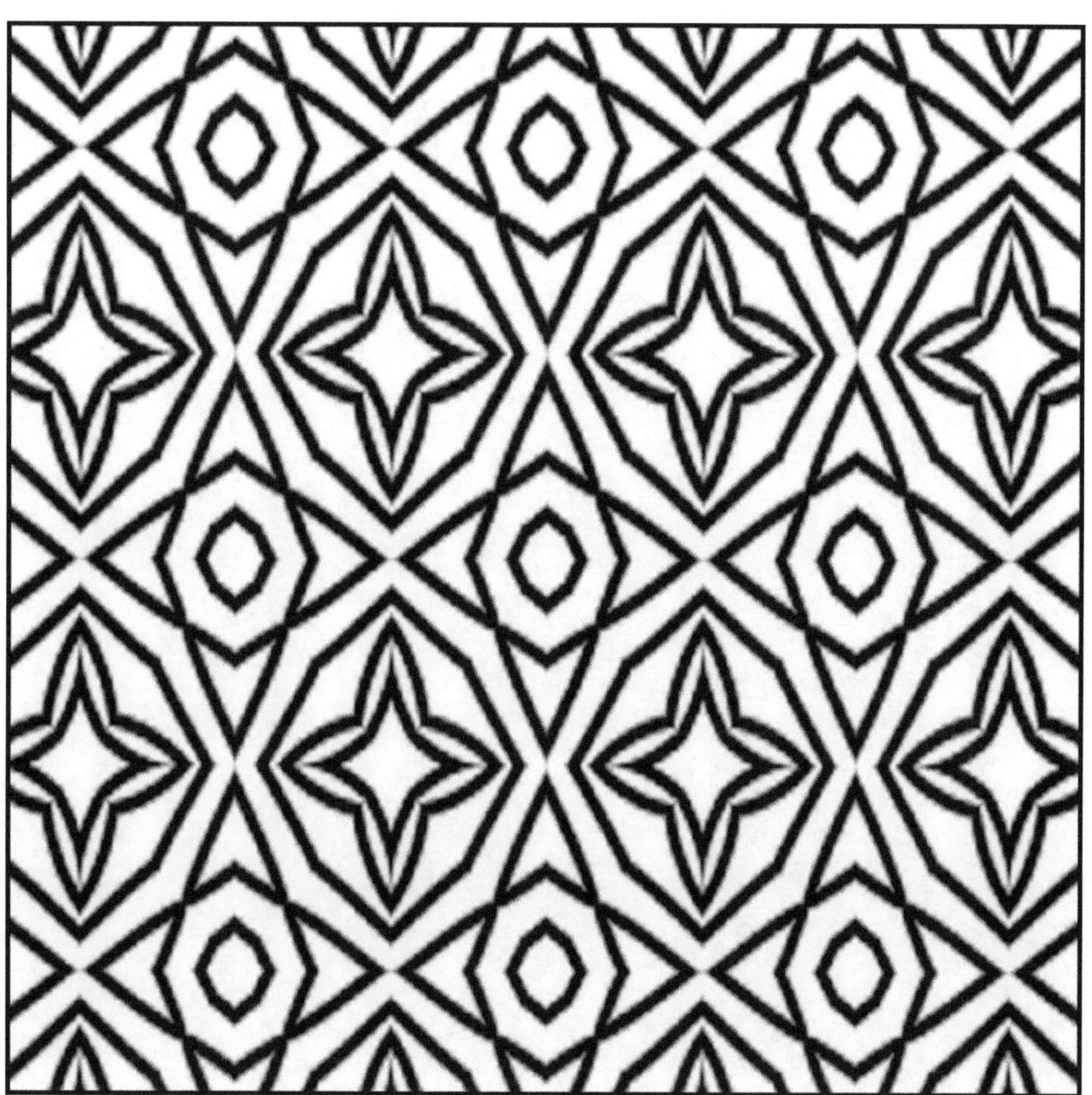

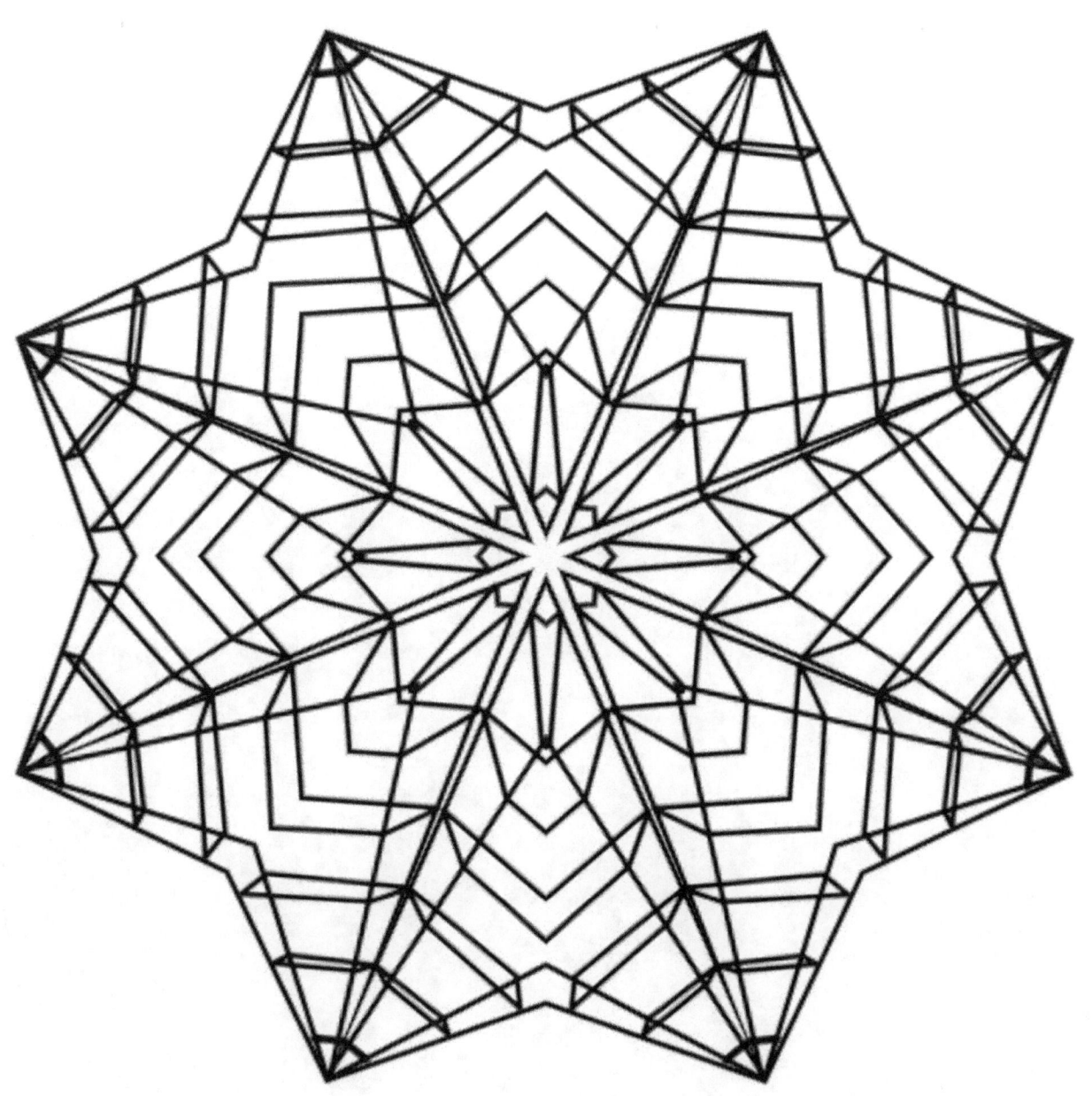

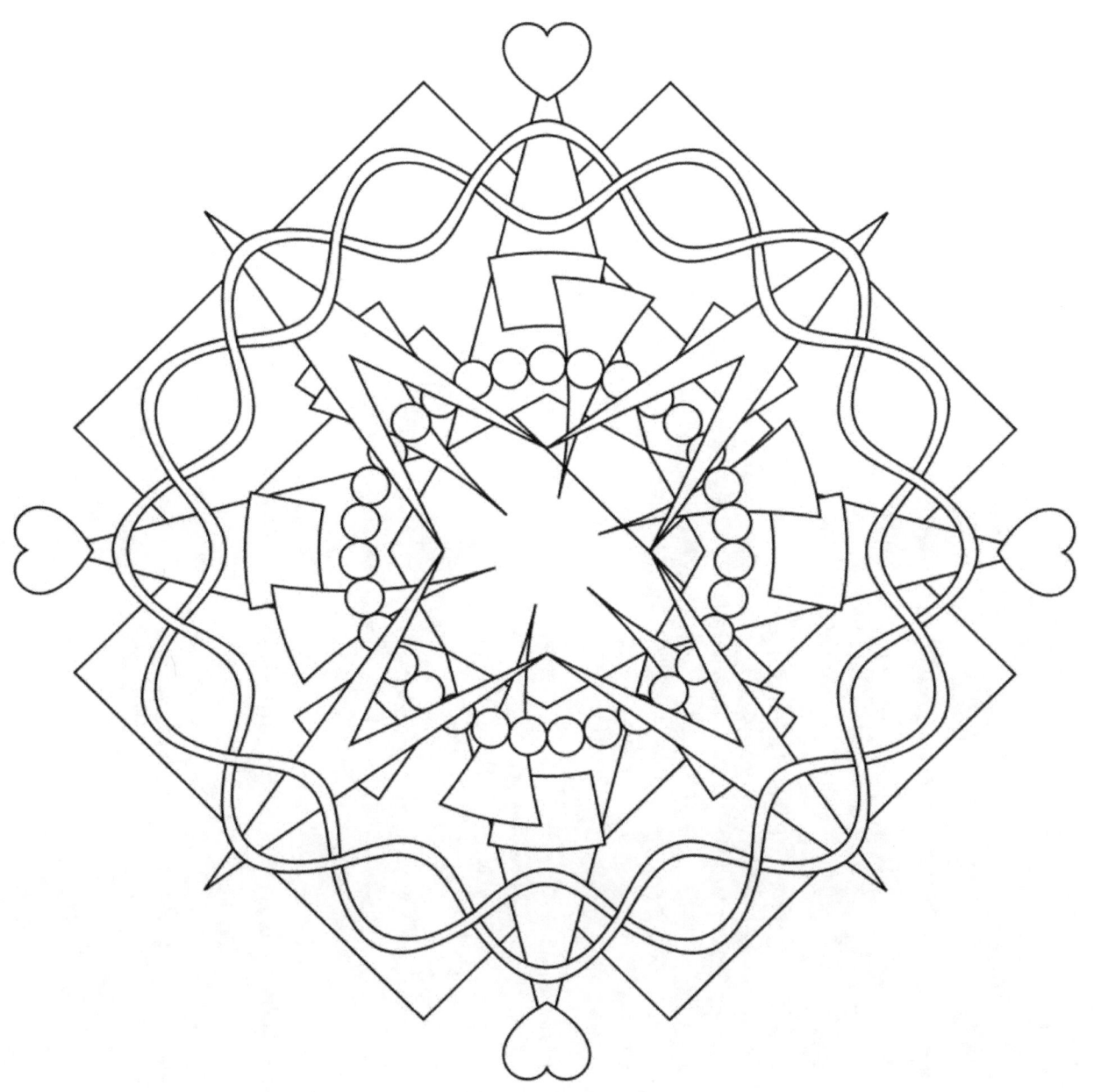

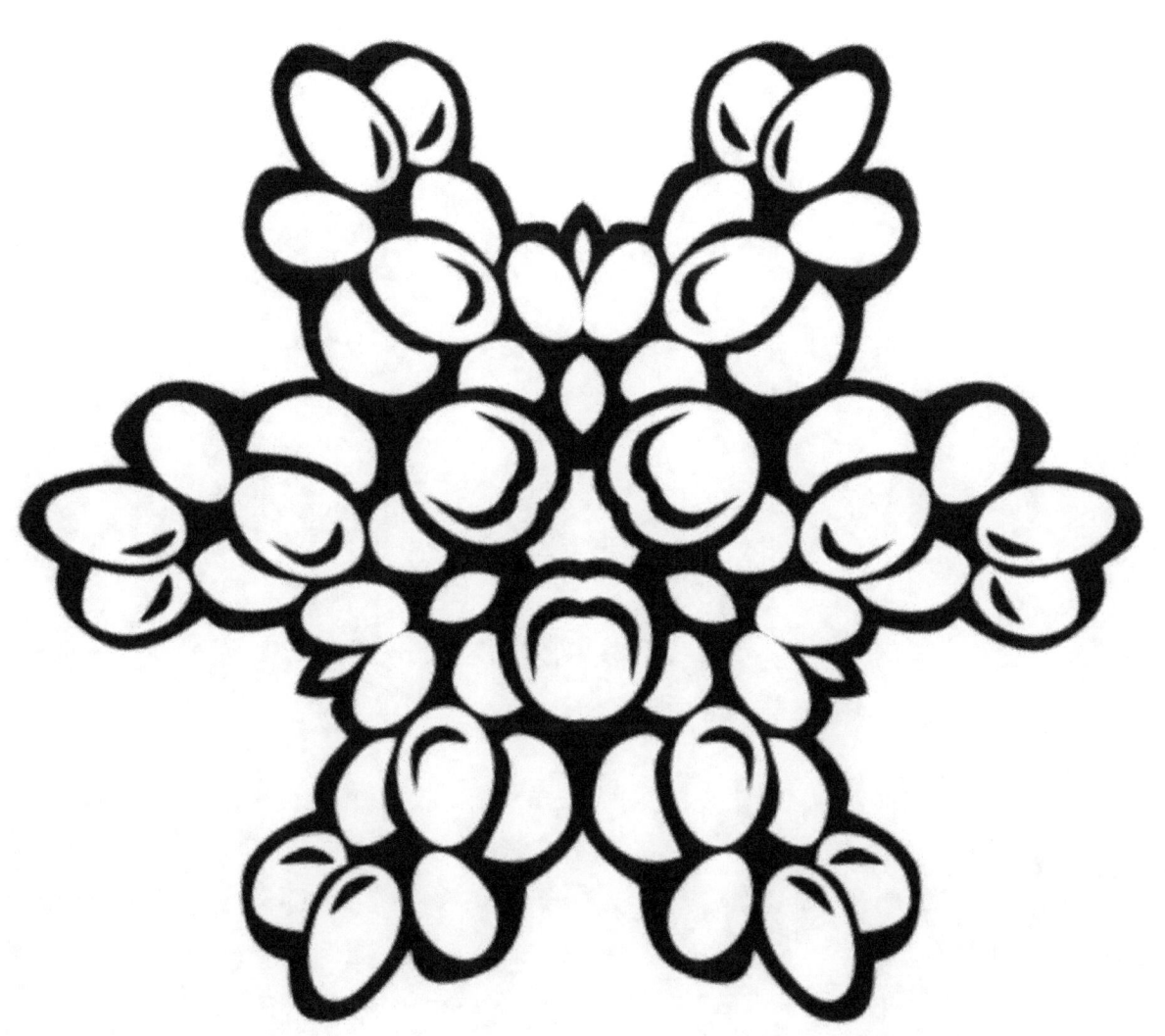

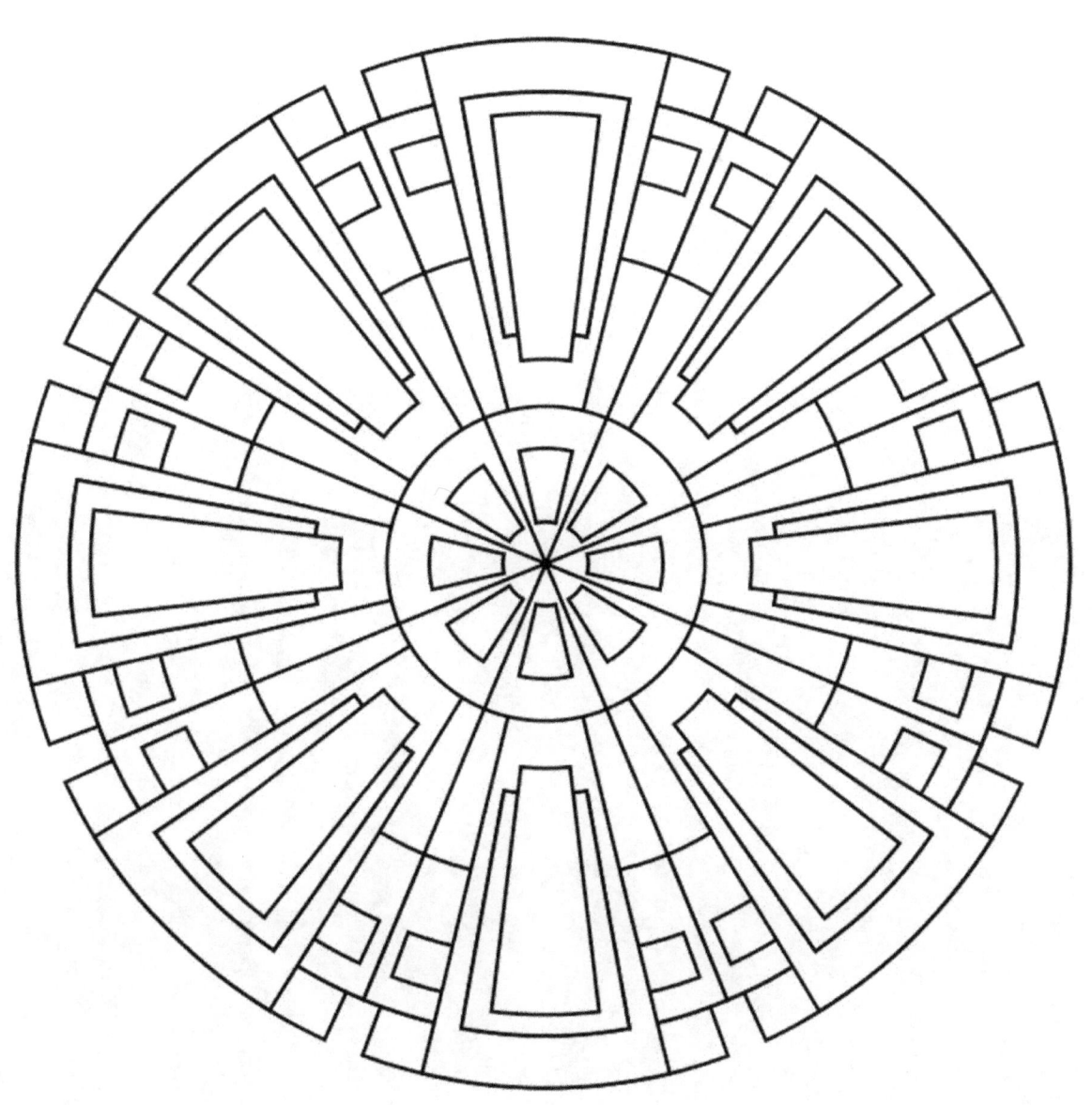

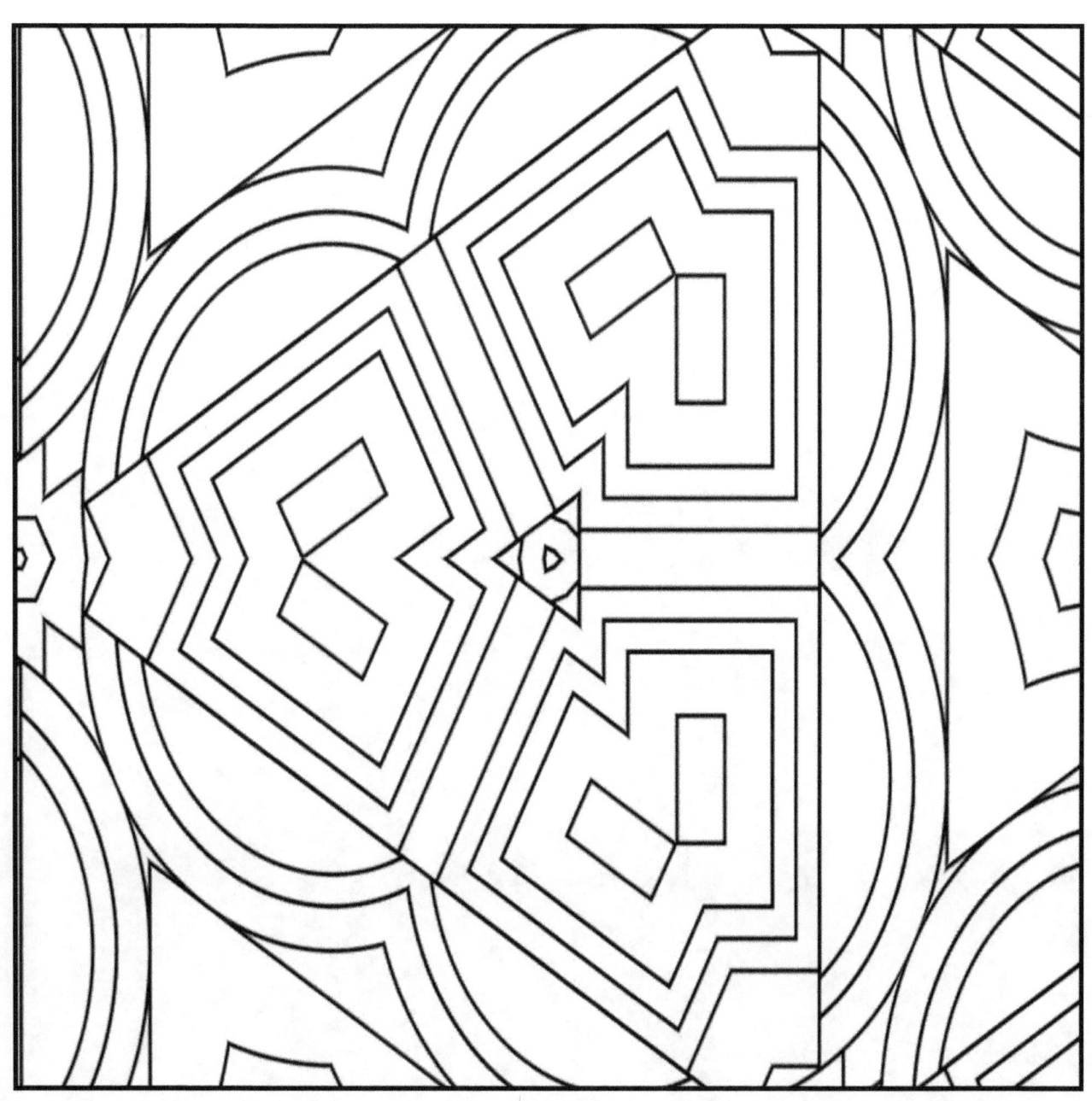

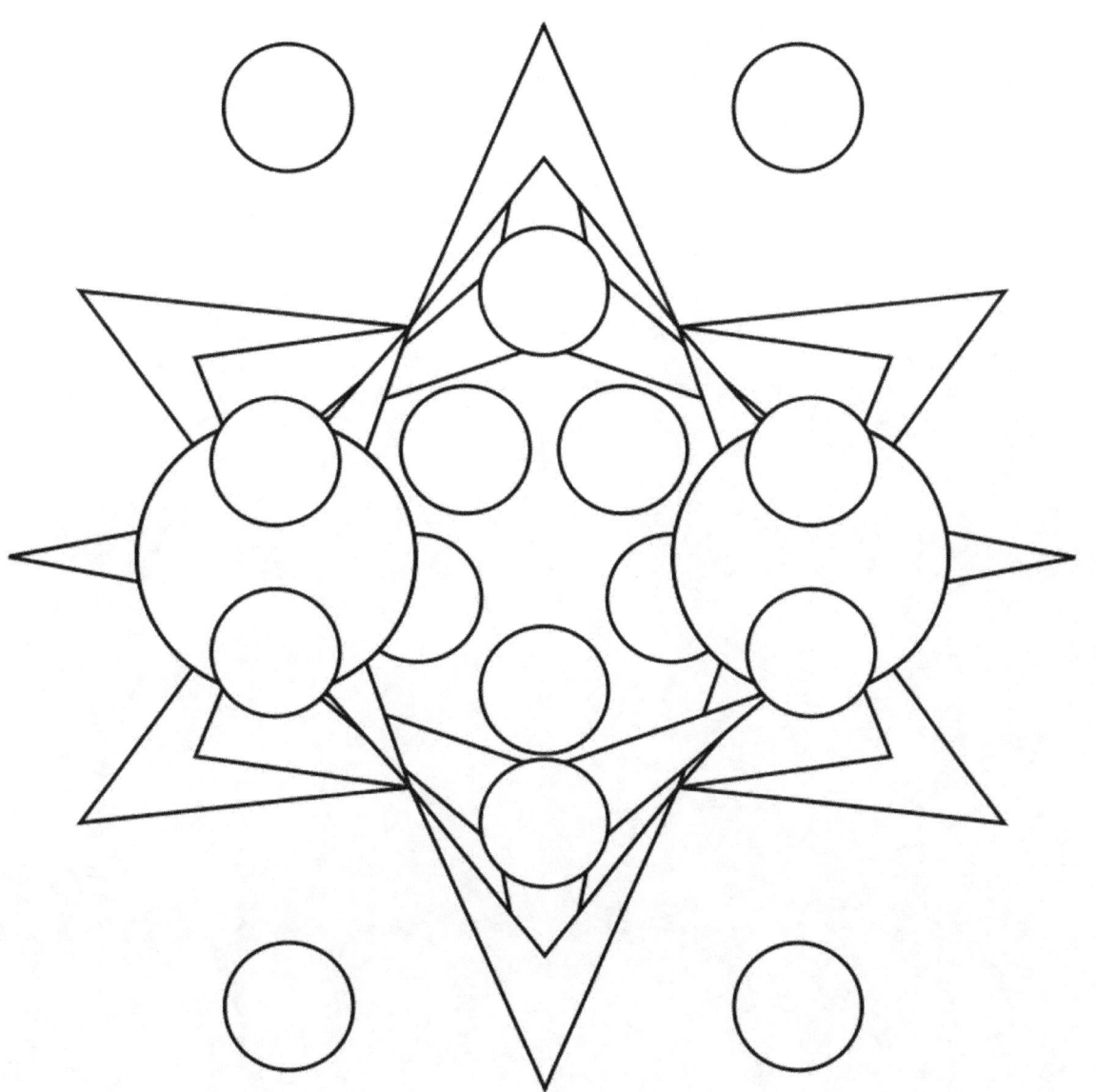

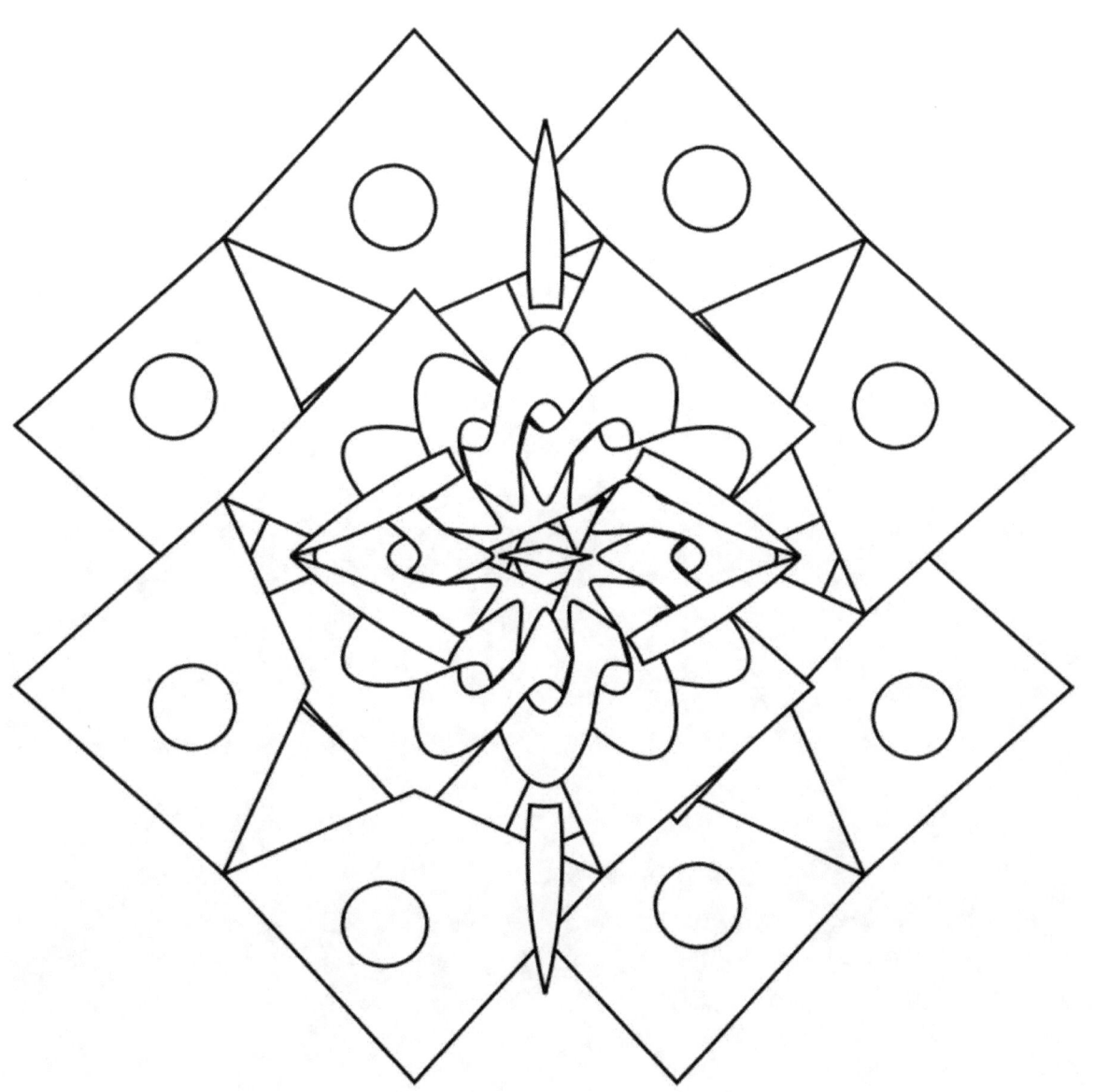

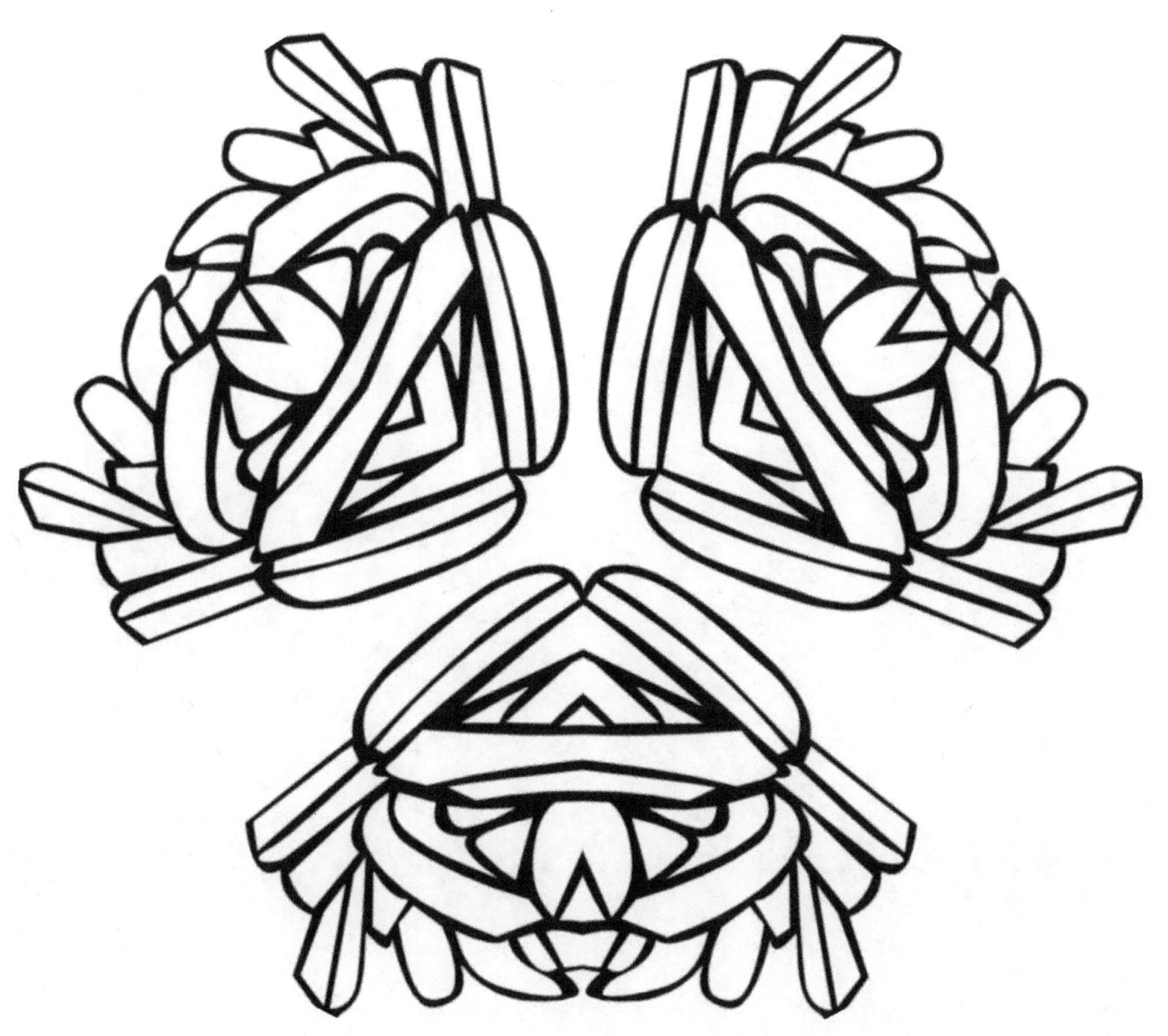

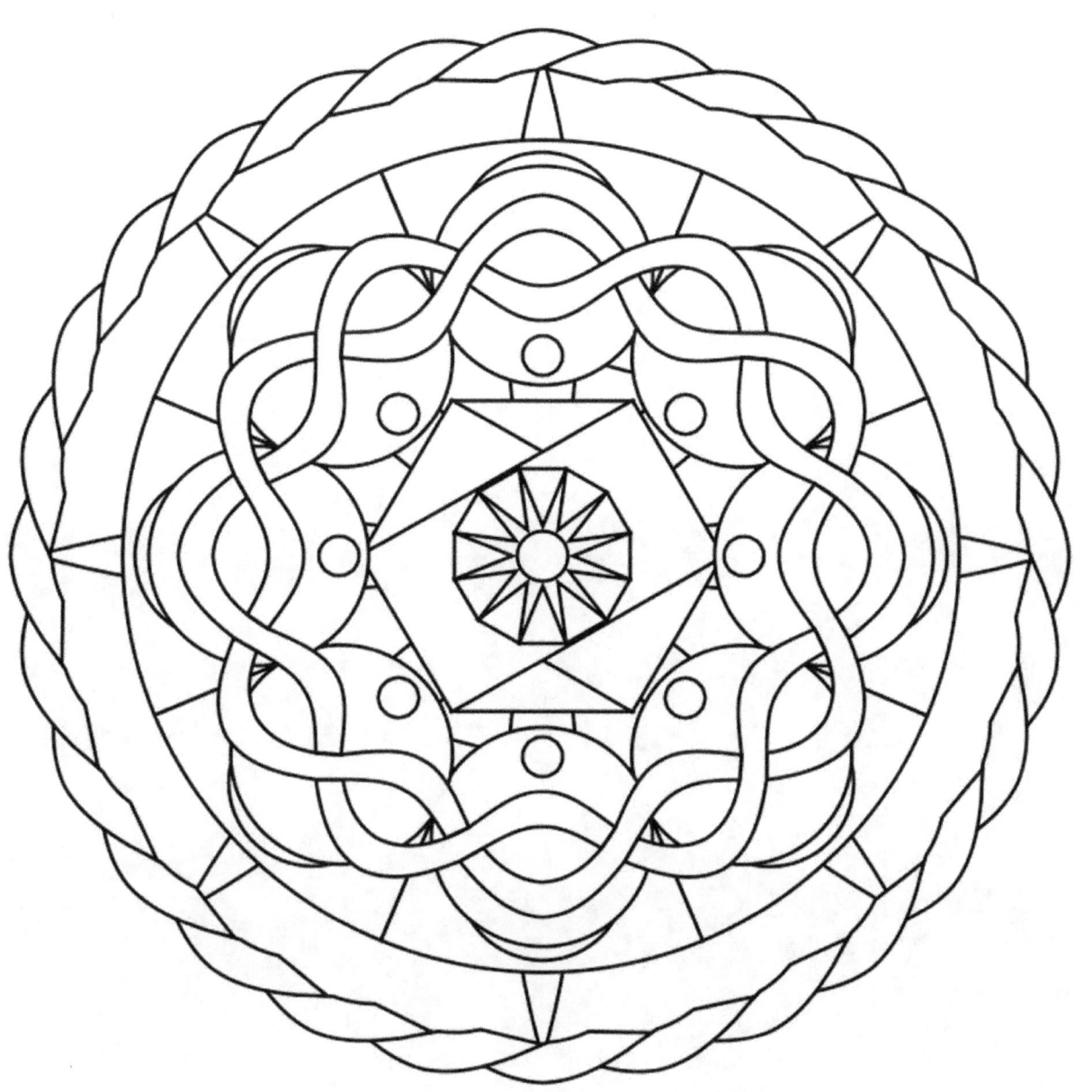

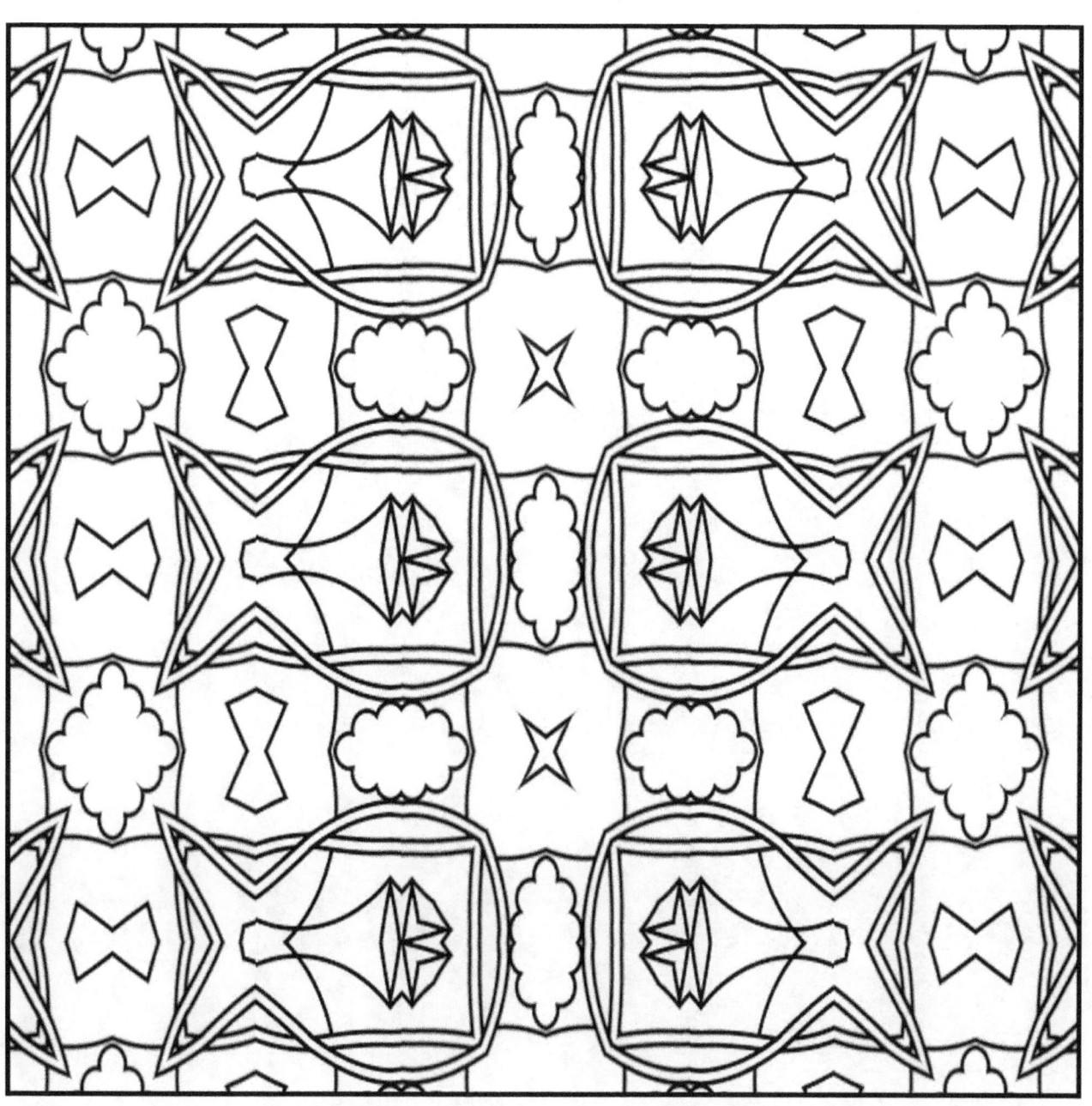

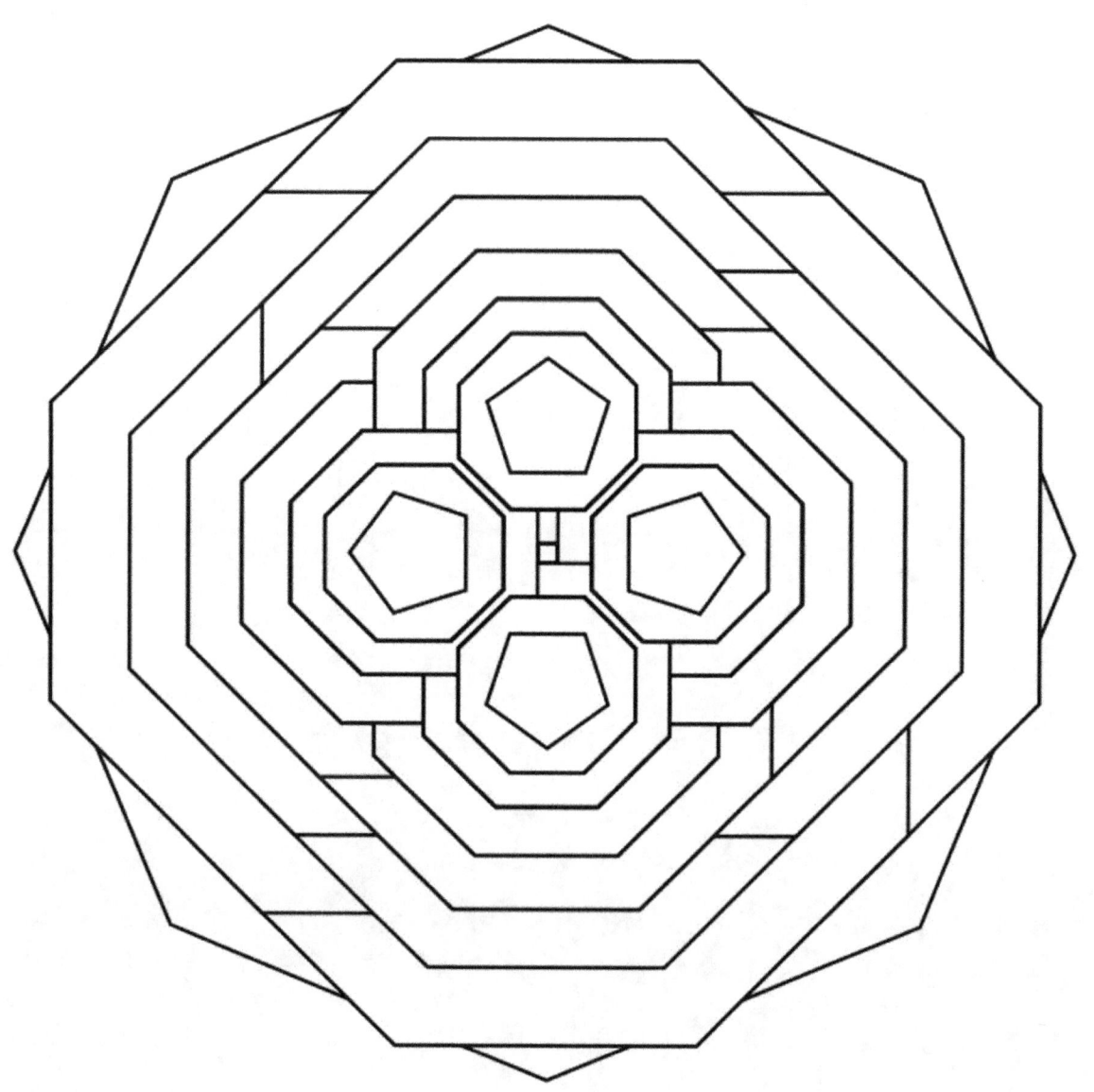

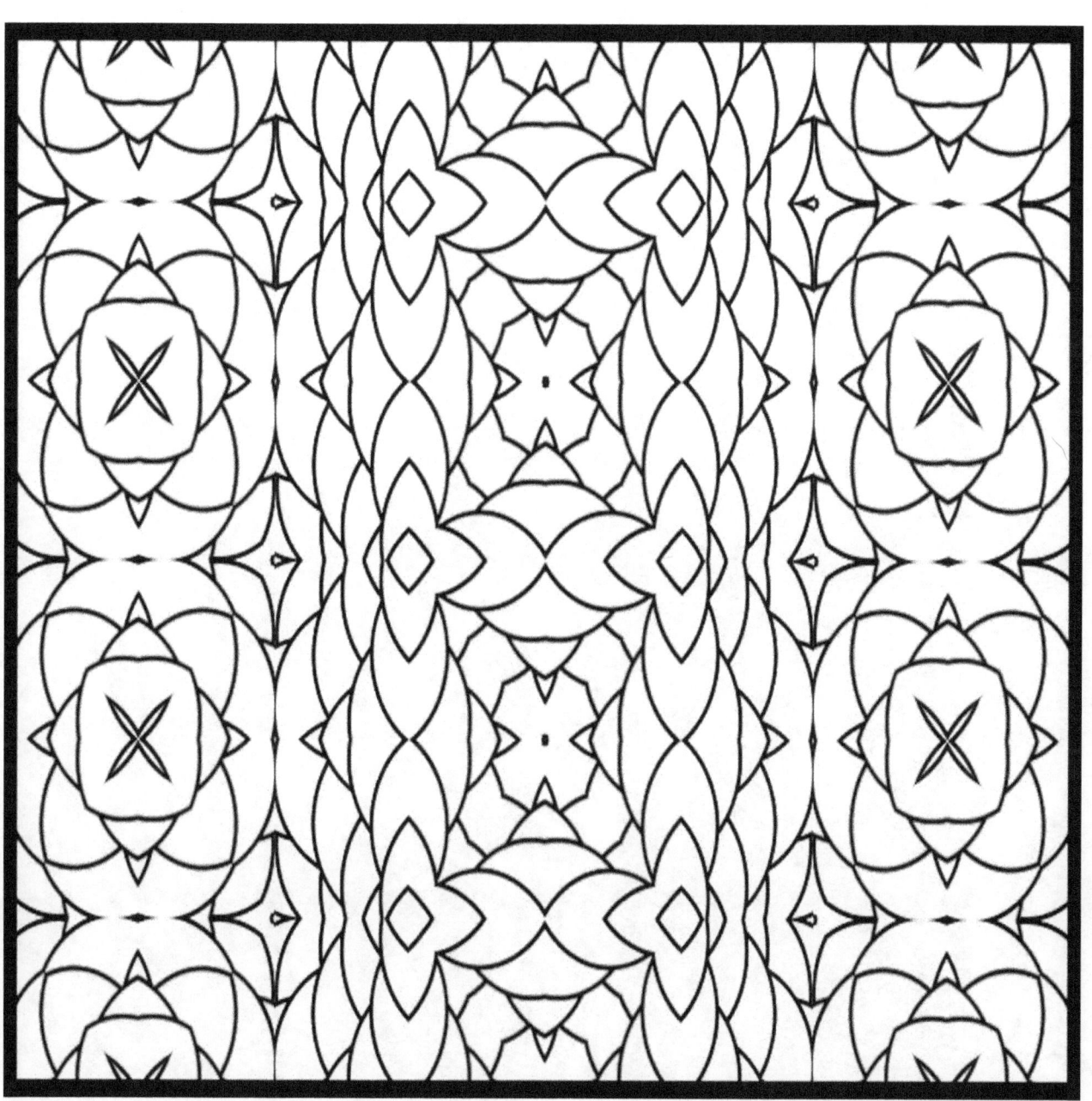

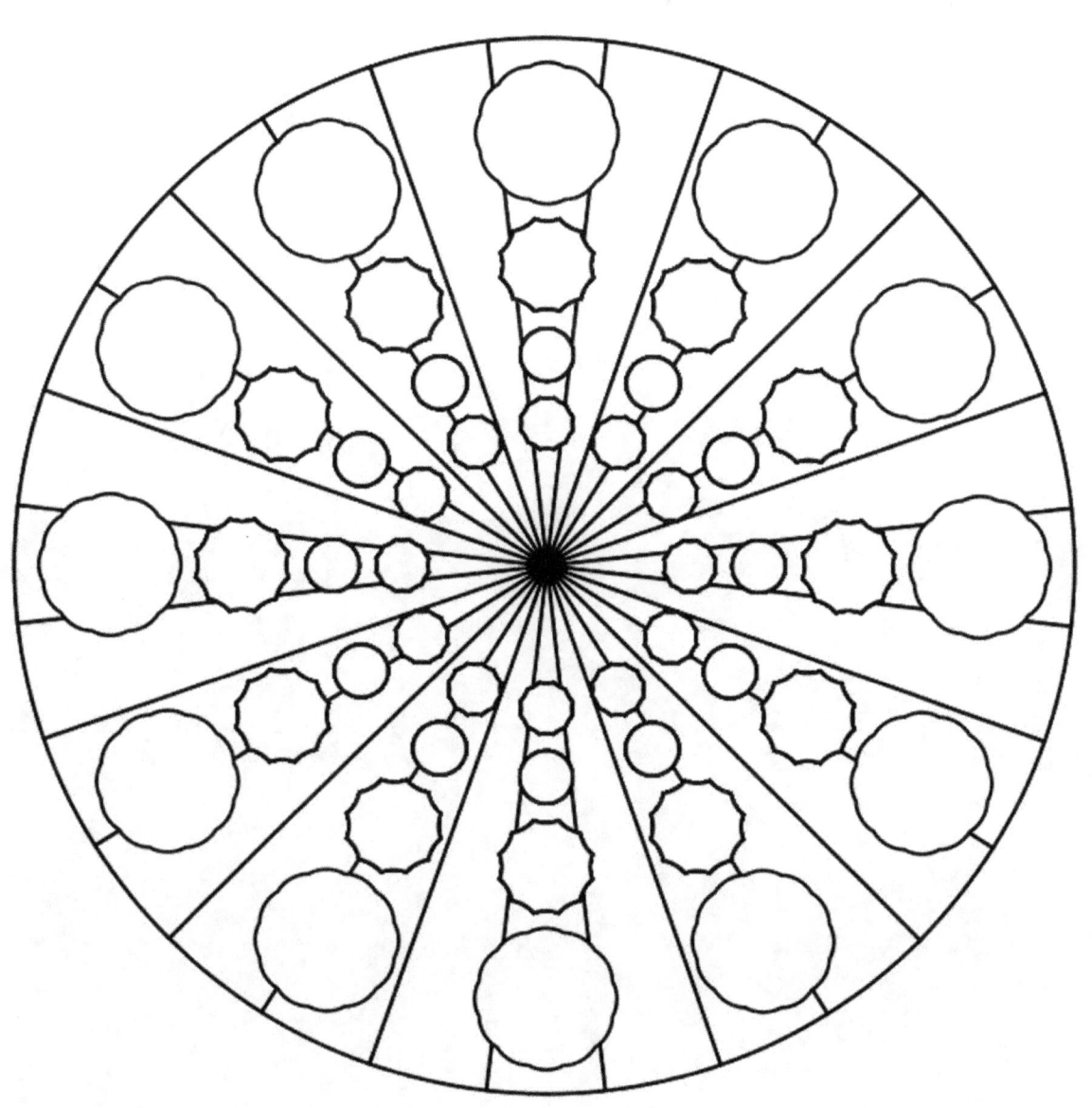

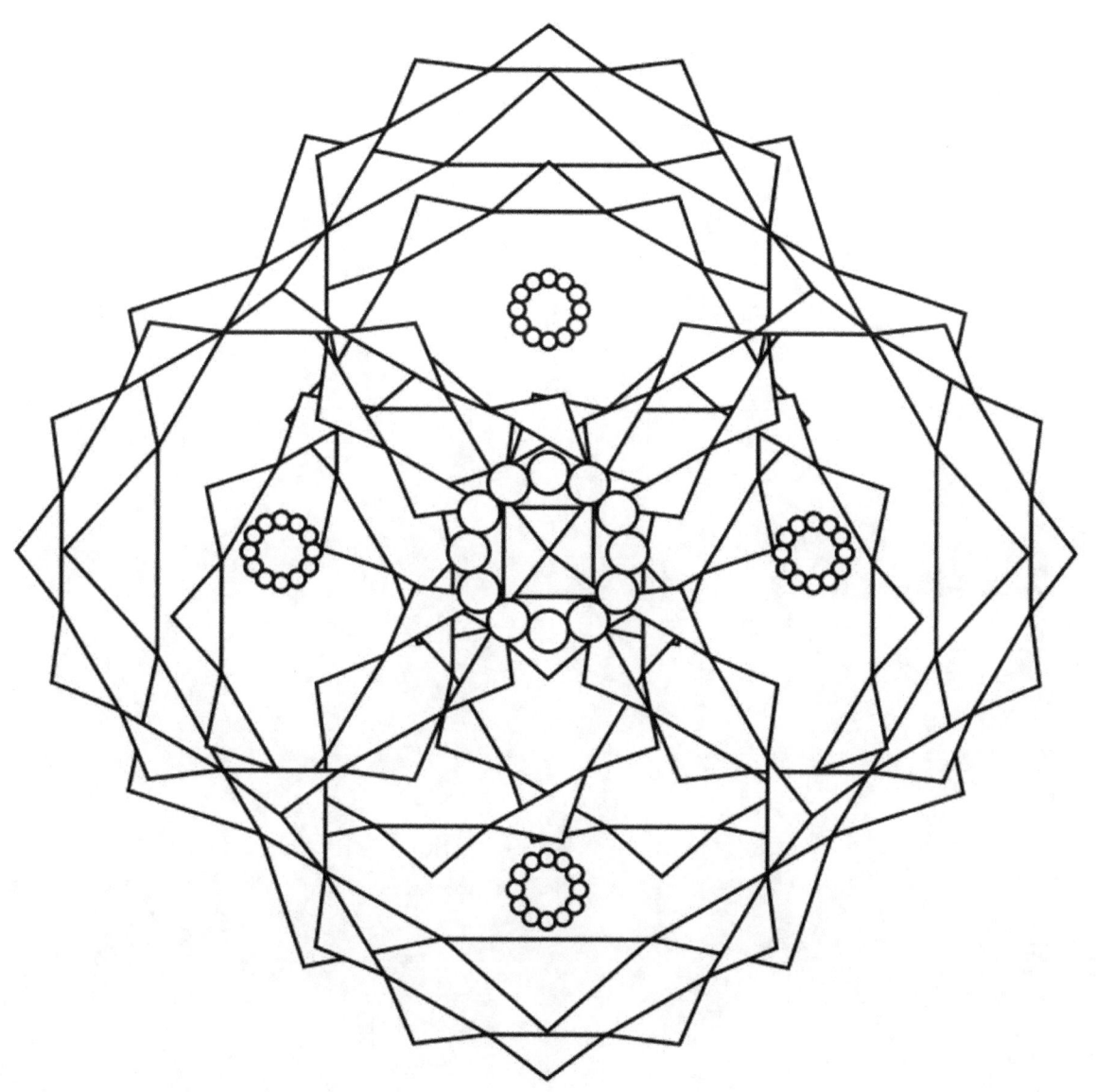

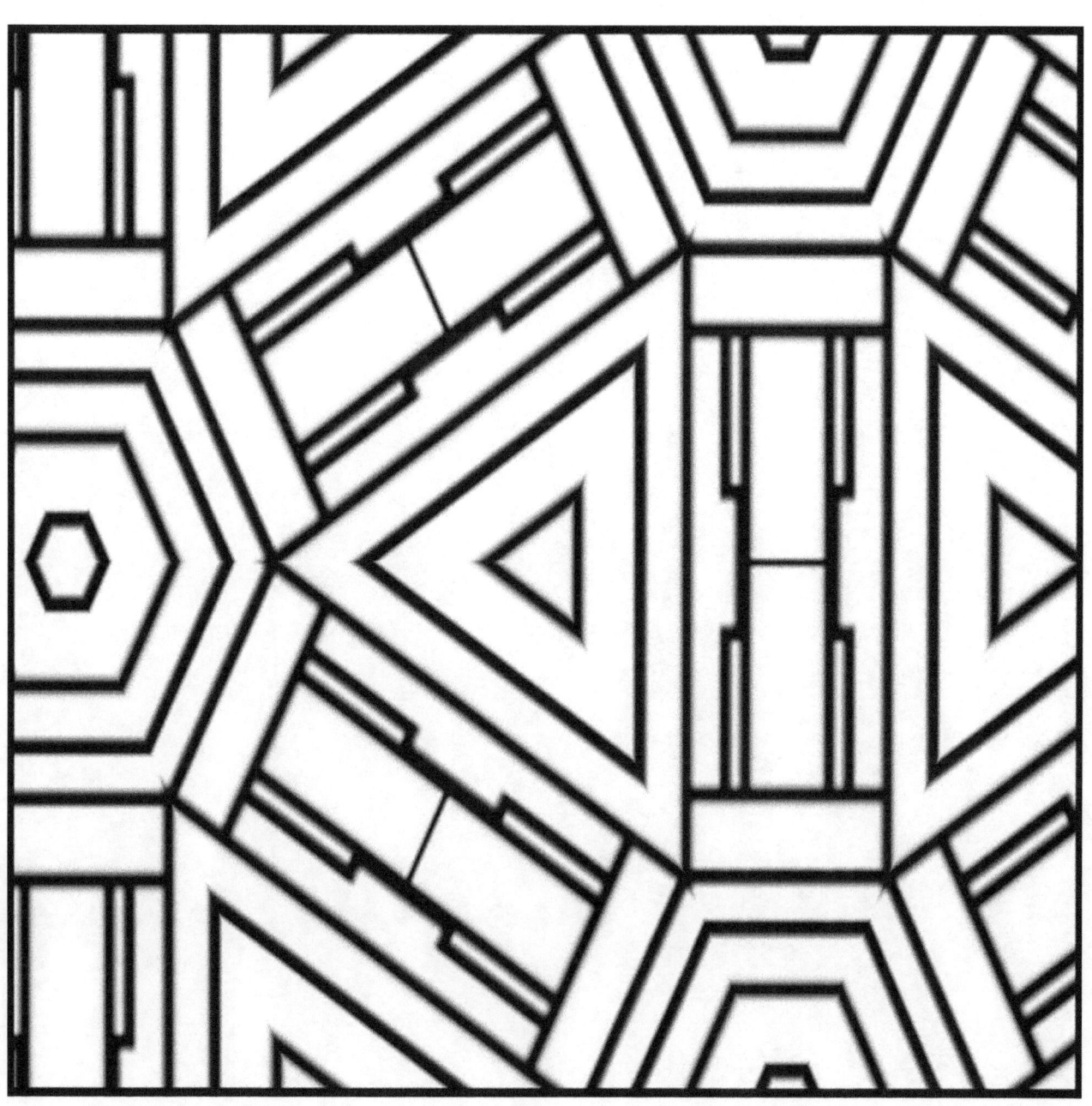

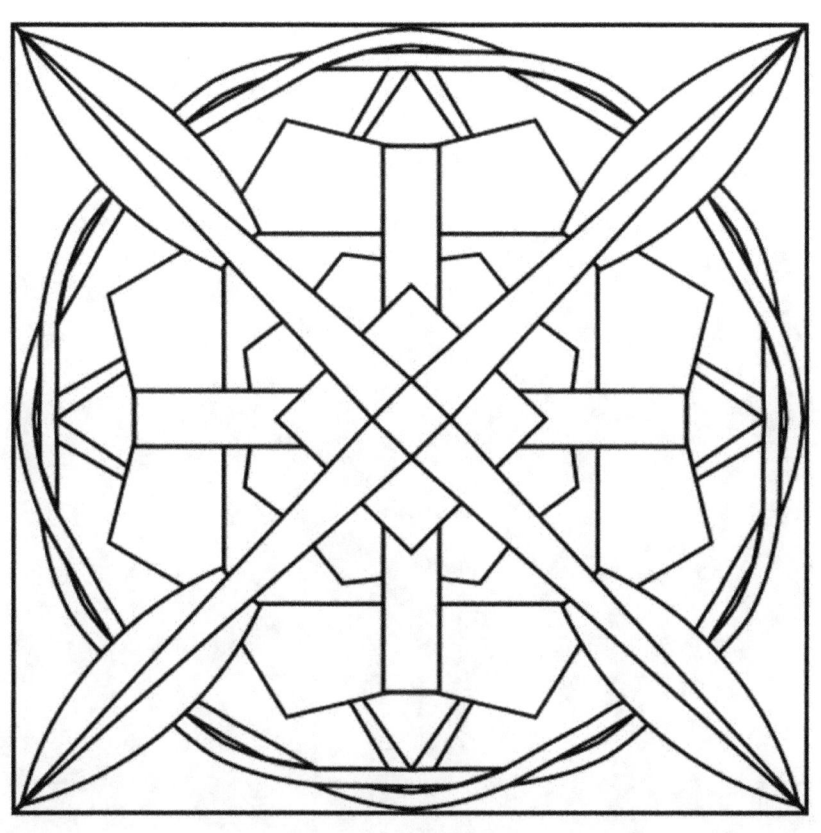

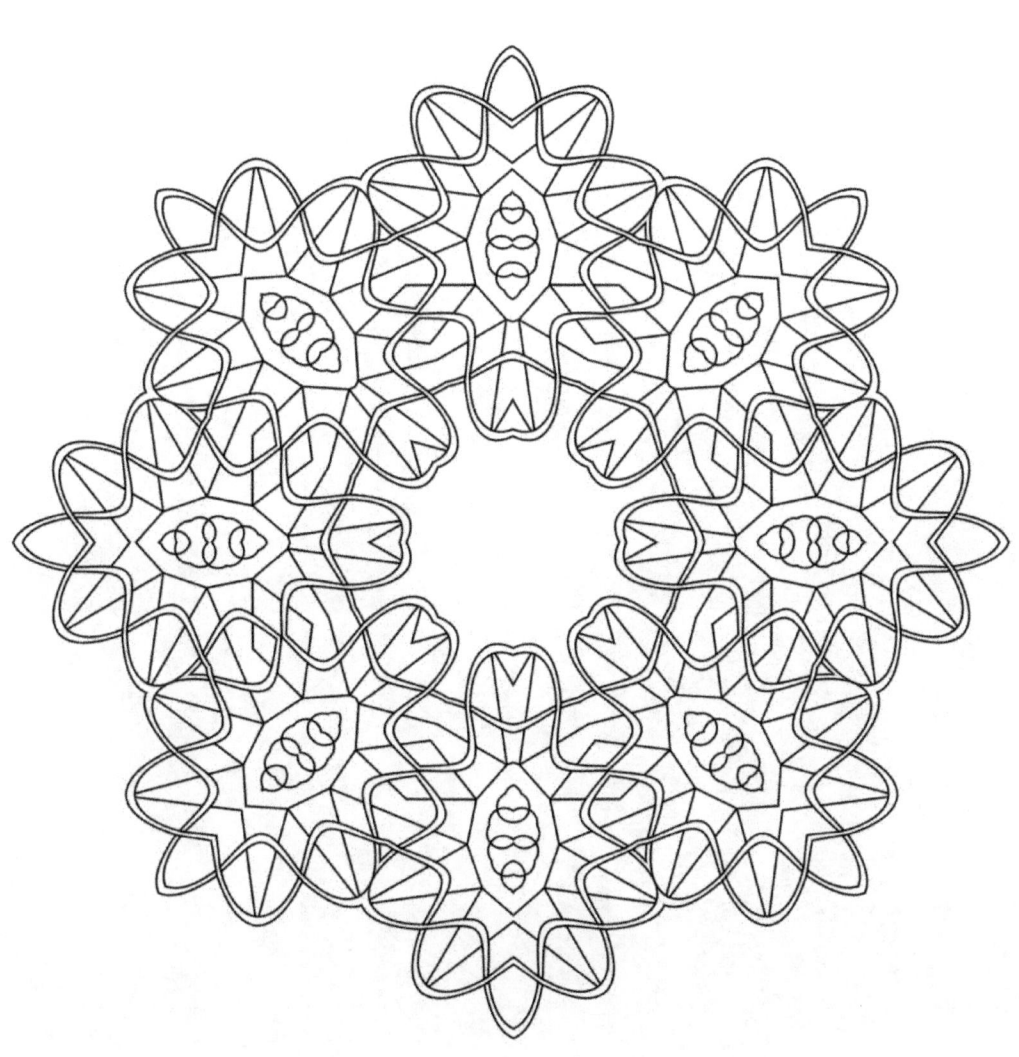

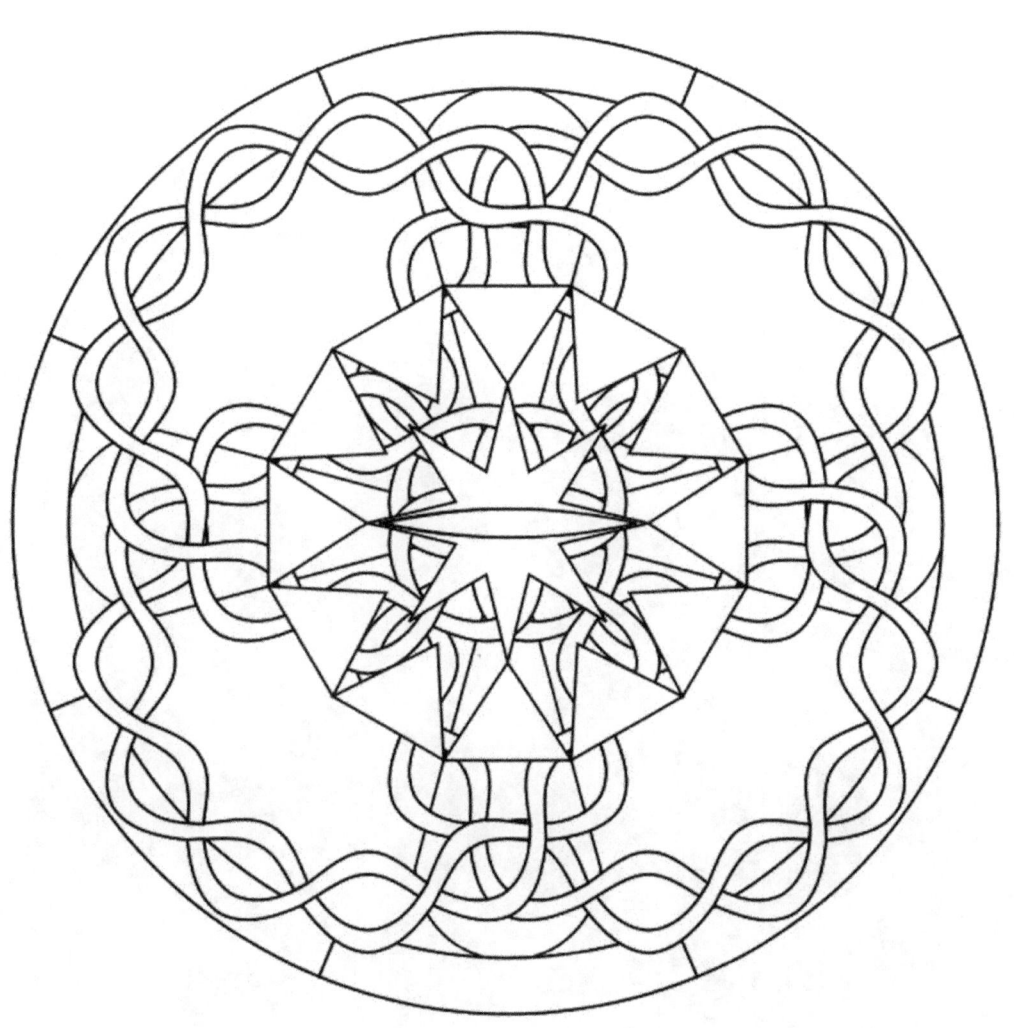

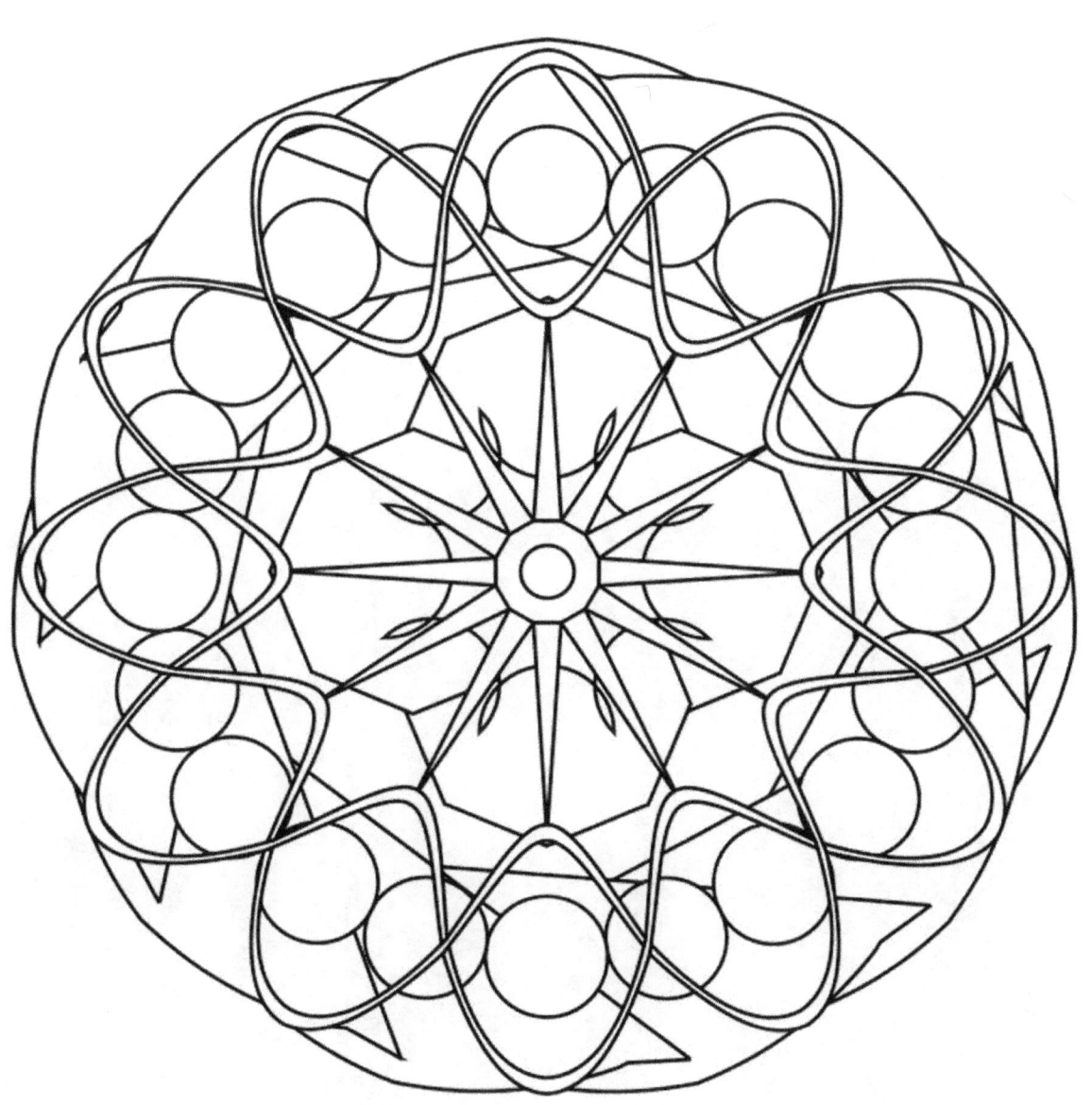

I hope you enjoyed coloring this book.

Please share your colored pages on my FaceBook page called Coloring Designs.

This is also a forum for leaving questions, comments, suggestions and congratulations.

THANK YOU FOR PURCHASING THIS BOOK!

You can find my other books on Amazon.com by typing RUTH MASON in the search box.

Please leave reviews!

I can always be contacted at favoritesofruthies@gmail.com

I look forward to hearing from you!

www.ingramcontent.com/pod-product-compliance
Lightning Source LLC
Chambersburg PA
CBHW080719190526
45169CB00006B/2430

* 9 7 8 1 5 2 3 8 4 3 4 1 1 *